Through it All

*A story of a surviving soul
and God's faithfulness*

By

Brigitte Kitenge

DeHoff Christian Bookstore
749 N. W. Broad Street
Murfreesboro, Tennessee 37129 USA

Page design and layout: Bonnie DeHoff Fakes
Images: Cover picture, Home Life magazine.
Cover Design: Creative Graphics, Lebanon, TN
Unless otherwise noted, scripture quotations are from the New King James Bible.
Printed in the United States of America

Publisher's Cataloging-in-Publication
Kitenge, Brigitte 1969—
Through it All / Brigitte Kitenge
Eighteen chapters, ill., 283 pages.
1. Autobiography 2. Survival story 3. Rwanda atrocities, 1994 4. Christian life and encouragement   5. Providence of God
    1. Kitenge, Brigitte 2. Title

ISBN: 975-1-933965-36-9

Dedication

To the woman whose heart God used to shape my destiny, when you took me in at the recommendation of my Grandmother, to become your house girl, you saw through the eyes of God. You saw more in me than how the world had defined me. You saw intelligence and you sent me to school, giving me an unparalleled education I would not otherwise have had. I am who I am today because of you and the opportunities you provided. All that I have been able to accomplish in education and in my career trace back to the initial faith you had in me. When I am privileged to help someone through my story or my ministry, it is because you first helped me. You have impacted the lives of everyone I come in contact with without even knowing it. You have no idea how far your influence has spread. Each of us is able to help someone in some way. You have helped many people you know not of in many ways you cannot imagine. I can look back now and see that your kindness and generosity came to me at the perfect time and in the perfect way for me to become all that God intended me to be. I dedicate this book to the woman who gave me the life I could never have had otherwise, and the courage to be able to live through it. Madame Leoncie Bongwa, my adopted and "God" mother, I can't say enough about you. You were the hand of God fashioning my life and I thank you for being there when I needed you and allowing God to use you.

Table of Contents

Dedication..3
Table of Contents..................................5
Acknowledgements...............................7
Introduction.......................................11
1. The Ache of April...........................15
2. Back to the Beginning.....................23
3. Hell on Earth.................................41
4. The Longest Night..........................55
5. On the Other Side of the Lake............69
6. All Gone Without Saying Goodbye.........81
7. Not Without My Daughters.................87
8. The Power of Hatred.......................105
9. Gathering My Broken Pieces..............117
10. Following the Shepherd...................153
11. Psalm 23....................................169
The Lord is My Shepherd....................169
He Makes Me Lie Down in Green Pastures..170
He Guides Me in the Paths of Righteousness173
I Will Fear No Evil.............................177
You Prepare a Table Before Me in the Presence of my Enemies...................................183
Surely Goodness and Mercy Shall Follow Me..188
And I will Dwell in the House of the Lord Forever..189
12. Welcome to America—The American Dream..191

13. The Wilderness.............................207
14. A Painful Lesson—Forgiveness...........233
15. Touch My Scars............................245
16. Hope Again................................255
17. Psalm 40...................................263
Through it All.................................277
Appendices/Map...............................279
Epilogue......................................283

Acknowledgements

Writing this book was a journey backward. I relived each step of my life in order to put it in writing. It wasn't an easy project.

I am thankful to the Lord Jesus Christ, who held my hand through it all, and to the many men and women He appointed on my rough road to guide me knowingly and unknowingly; they were perfect tools.

To my four daughters: Arlette, Axelle, Anita, and Arrielle, if some angels in heaven are missing wings I know where they are. My four wings, you carried me, you kept me high above discouragement, above adversity, and you made me mount tirelessly like an eagle. With you I soar higher every day.

To Pastor Pat and Amy Hood, Senior Pastor of Life Point Church, Smyrna, Tennessee, that day in 2006 at Starbucks, when you and Amy said in unison, "We can do this," and paid those many thousand dollars to bring back our house from a foreclosure, without forgetting other situations when you stood not only as a shepherd, but as a brother in Christ, I saw the hand of God through you. Pastor Pat, you will always stand tall in my heart.

To Judy and Brian Wilcox, M.D., when I came to America in 2000, I met many people. They came in and out of my life, but you chose to stay. Your unconditional love, endless support, and opportunities you gave to me and my daughters made it possible to keep moving. May you be rewarded for each act of kindness; each burden you took off my shoulders, and for standing by me through it all. I will never be able thank you enough.

To Debbie and Marty Martinez, you left your finger prints on my heart when you allowed the Lord to use you during one of the dark seasons in my life. I am thankful for God's wisdom and your obedience.

To Judy Vance, for believing that the story of my life needed to be put in proper English for all to know how God brought me through it all, your recommendation to Bonnie Fakes made this book readable.

To Mylinda Solley, if the incarnation is real, you must be one of my sisters. Words can't express how grateful I am for the true friendship and the sisterhood you gave me. You are a gracious blessing from the Lord.

To Cindy Sproles and the Ashville Christian Writers team, when you granted me that scholarship to the three-day Christian writers conference, you allowed me to dream again.

To Bonnie Fakes, my retired English teacher friend, the spaceship candidate who cheated death that day in 1986, for you were not done yet, how can I thank you for the many weekends sacrificed, translating my Frenglish into the American language? You encouraged me to complete the manuscript and worked tirelessly to fix it. I still don't understand why you do what you do. There are not many people of your kind in the world.

To a man who may not want to read this book, my former socio study teacher, life partner, the father of my four daughters; for journeying with me for those many years, I forgave you and I hope you can believe and receive it.

To my heroes, all the women survivors of all that horror, and to those out there who are hurting, desperate, and still looking for a safe place — when I tell my story, I tell yours. Don't give up! Keep moving one step at a time. God is with you through it all.

Introduction

In the midst of April 1994, I had been on the run for days--running for my life. There was a death sentence hanging over my head, and those of my tribe; the voice on the radio saying, "There is no escape for those cockroaches--finish them all." This had been the slogan for weeks and it haunted me day and night. It brought an unbearable pain to my stomach and my knees were shaking. My fear was going to give me away. I must fake it until I make it!

I was lonely and lost, wounded physically and emotionally, and totally exhausted. I sat on a bus, together with my killers, like a sheep riding with the butcher. I knew with certainty that there was no escape. I was young—just 22 years old—once full of energy, dreams, and hope for a bright future, but now I found myself on the road to nowhere. I sat on the bus through the night waiting for my hour to come. The night lasted longer than usual. There was no need of hope and no use for faith, because I believed my fate was already decided.

That night, I knew that if I made it through, I would write this book. I would write it out of my own need to put into words some of the most important things I have come to believe and experience, and I would write this book to help other people who might one day find themselves in a similar situation. I would write it for all those people who wanted to go on believing, but whose anger toward God made it hard for them to hold on to their faith and be comforted by the general knowledge of "GOD". I would write it for all those people who raise the question, "Where is God when I am hurting?" while their faith is being tested and for those whose desperate need to find meanings, lead them to blame themselves for their suffering and persuade themselves that they somehow deserved it.

Through It All is the book you are reading and it is my memoir. It is the same testimony that I have given in churches and magazines, only this time, I focus less on what I went through, and more on how God brought me through, and how He led me out of my troubles.

My friend, this story is not a fiction: it is a tale of a surviving soul; a story of grace and God's faithfulness. I am a simple woman who has been hurt by life, and I wanted to write a book that could be given to any other person who has been hurt by life, by death, by illness or loss, by rejection or disappointment, and who knows in his heart that if there is justice in this world, that he deserves better. What can God mean to you and me? Where can we turn for strength and hope? If you are like me, if you want to believe in God's goodness and fairness, but find it hard because of the things that have happened to you and to people you love and care about. If this book helps you to do that, then I will have succeeded in distilling some blessings out of my pain and tears.

This is my story as I remember it. Each detail of it is engraved in my soul and it is true. It is the story of a lifetime, and it is mine. It is my prayer that as you read the pages of this book, hope will come alive in your heart. I hope you will see that hurts, pains, and losses need not destroy us, but rather can shape and bring a better understanding of life, along with a greater wisdom and compassion when scanned through the light of the love of God. I pray that you will gain a deeper courage to continue the journey and enjoy the different seasons you are going through with hearts full of gratitude, knowing that every season has a beginning and an end, that no matter how long the night might last, the morning will break and the sun will shine again, when you allow the master of all seasons to carry you through it all.

Chapter One—The Ache of April

A Season for Everything

A wise man once said:
> "To everything there is a season,
> A time for every purpose under heaven:
> A time to be born and a time to die;
> A time to plant, and a time to pluck up
> what is planted;
> A time to kill and a time to heal;
> A time to break down and a time to build
> up;
> A time to weep and a time to laugh;
> A time to mourn and a time to dance;
> A time to gain and a time to lose...
> *Ecclesiastes 3:1-8*

For some of us it is difficult to understand the wisdom behind the preacher's (Solomon, the son of David) writing. This man, who had it all, taught us that nothing lasts: good, evil, sweet, sour, night or day. "This too shall pass away," he said.

In his wisdom, Solomon observed the cycle of life and left us with something to remind us that *nothing* is permanent. When we are caught up in a season, no matter how it looks, it will pass; success will pass, failure will pass, summer will pass and winter will not last forever. The cycle of life is made by different seasons; some are better to live through, and some are positively dreadful. Without seasons, life would be boring; without seasons, we would not sow seeds and harvest them; we would starve and die of hunger. Without seasons, we would have no purpose for waking up and facing a new day.

The word *time* has two meanings in the Hebrew language:
Time (quantity, duration of time, which may be a point, a lapse, a span, a period). This is *Chronos*; it has to do with chronology and can be counted on a clock or calendar.
There is also:

Time (quality of time, opportune time, set time, appointed time, due time, definitive time, seasonable time, and proper time for an action). This is *Kairos.*

Chronos denotes time in quantity--extend or length of time, while *kairos* describes time as the appointed time in quality.

For instance, when Jesus told His disciples that it is not for them to know the times or the seasons in Acts 1:7, He was talking of time chronos, but in Colossians 3:5, we are told to walk in wisdom toward those who are outside, redeeming the time--we are talking of time kairos.

Chronos tells what day it is; kairos suggests the kind of time. Kairos tells of special happenings occurring during the time frame of chronos. Seasons (kairos) are made by different times (chronos).

When we are aware of the season we are in, we will not be anxious or bored by the length of time it takes to pass through it. It has a fixed beginning and an end. There is a great risk when we do not take time to discern the season we are going through. When we walk in ignorance, we open a door for the enemy to show us the length (chronos) of time and the quantity of pain it brings. Then, instead of enjoying the journey, we become prisoners of time and pain. We can easily miss the whole reason for the season.

How could Elijah be so terribly depressed as to pray, "It is enough, now Lord, take my life." (1

Kings 19:4)? As we face different trying situations and enter difficult conflicts, we come to understand why God allows His people to be put in these situations. Because we have walked in similar places, we become more compassionate, rather than being overcritical.

There is relief in discovering that we are walking paths that others have traveled. Once we take a close look at their lives, we can clearly see that they were walking. They didn't stop in the difficulties; they were on a journey. It was a season. It is very important to count the cost of the journey and understand the season we are in before we adventure. Most of us have found ourselves on a journey with no clue as to where it would end.

Elijah, the mighty man of God—the powerful prophet who called fire down and performed miracles and wonders, who saw the power of the living God operating through him, who spoke on behalf of the God of Israel—had lived through a season of victory. Suddenly, the seasons changed and he forgot the remaining part of the journey. No one lives forever on the top of the hill; there is a time to get down in the valley. In fact, there is no way to get from one hill top to another without going through a valley.

I learned that life is made up of a series of new

beginnings, although they will be different from the ones we knew before. My friend, I don't know about you, but like Elijah, I have lived through all these seasons and discovered that each time I get an opportunity to say "hello" to a season of victory, I must also be willing to say "goodbye" as well, because "this too shall pass."

I learned that we must be willing to *let go* before we can embrace again. I must admit that all seasons are not the same and I am glad that this is the way it is.

T.S. Eliot once said, "What we call the beginning is often the end; and to make an end is to make a beginning. The end is where we start from." Every season has a beginning and an end. The length of time as we measure it, between beginning and end, may be fractions of a second, or thousands of years.

Some seasons left me so joyful that it was difficult to let them go, and some left such a dark scar on my heart that I still can't believe they are over.

Every April reminds me of my vulnerability-- my losses and endless grief and carries the truth that my life was touched so profoundly that nothing will ever be the same. The painful feelings of walking away from all I had ever known, the fear of embracing the unknown, the grief of my many losses, touched numerous areas of my life. I found myself fighting, avoiding, struggling with and being angry or confused about the many forms of loss that I experienced, such as being uprooted from one place to another, or being on the run for many years.

I experienced both betrayal and rejection. There was always the inner question, "Why me"? I kept thinking why should I experience hardship over and over? Then I developed an attitude that said life will always be a hardship and that nothing good would ever happen to me.

In Rwanda, we have four agricultural seasons, but when I was growing up, I noticed only two seasons: the rainy or the sunny season. The weather is so pleasant that the Belgians who colonized us, called Rwanda the "Land of everlasting spring". The vegetation is always green, but the month of April is rainy and it gets pretty nasty when prolonged rains are falling down in villages. During her story telling, Grandma told us that our Father passed away in a car crash during one of the worst heavy, rainy seasons, while coming back from work. It was in the midst of April back in the 1970's. She also said that a few years later, Mom got sick and passed away and that happened to be in April also. She told us that the whole time Mom was sick, it was raining, but on the day she passed away, the rain stopped, miraculously giving them time to bury her.

Because of these events, I always had a bad feeling about the month of April. Since I had had chronic asthma, April has always weighed heavily on my health. Soon, it was to leave a scar on my heart also. All the time I saw April rain as if God, the angels, and all the hosts of heaven were sad and crying over my situation. The dark sky and heavy clouds have always had a negative impact on my health and the feeling in my heart. April of 1994 wasn't any different. It was a normal month with a regular routine in every way. I could not have predicted that this April was going to shatter my heart.

Although that season of my life was difficult, I would like to think that it softened my heart rather than hardening it. I lost everything and everyone. I woke up in the midst of a holocaust. I spent years on the run seeking a safe place to make a home again. I learned that life holds many promises, growths, and surprising treasures. I dedicated my life to finding them.

This period of my life was a season of facing loss and growing because of it. It was painful because it stretched not only my body, but my mind and my attitude about life and the exploration of options ahead of me. I was on my own and had to walk the trail of life all by myself. Today, as I look back to those dark years, I am thankful that though I thought I was all alone, now I can see the footsteps of God were always by my side.

This was one of the Seasons. There will always be places in my life bruised by the events of April: loneliness, betrayal, bitterness, anger and so many losses I have experienced, but I am thankful for where I am today. In America, April is a season of new beginnings—it's spring! There were many other seasons in my life and as I share my journey with you, I will touch on these seasons, hoping that you will be able to see yourself and the season you are in. I pray that you will not be hard on yourself, and do not curse the season because it seems dark and tough, or because you don't understand all the "why's." Remember there is a reason for that season in your life.

Chapter Two—Back to the Beginning

In October of 1988, I married my former professor. He taught social studies and was my teacher twice a week. He was a very handsome and intelligent young man, newly graduated from the university. He was just finished getting his Bachelor in Economics and Rural Development, in Zaire/Congo. We moved to Kigali, the capital city of Rwanda, and our first daughter was born in September of 1989. She brought us joy and a sense of maturity. We devoted our time and efforts to building our young family, always working hard to make ends meet. Leon left his teaching job and became a salesman and I got busy with the baby and school. By this time, my dream was to get a higher education in order to become a lawyer. The school was only a few streets from our house, so I was able to spend time with my daughter between classes. My family was very proud of me and my brothers and sisters were very supportive.

My husband had a good job and we had a nice home and car. We were able to afford a new life in the capital city of Rwanda; we were both committed to fulfilling our potential. I was full of energy, ambitions, and dreams. What I didn't know was that my dreams were about to be interrupted.

For a while, tensions had been building up between the political parties. There were militias and rumors of war in the country, especially in the city where we lived. From 1990 on, fear was in the air we breathed; there were sporadic killings and kidnappings. Who knew who would be next? It was said that for security matters, anybody could be picked up for questioning and those so gone never came back.

It became clear that a certain category of people was targeted: Tutsi who were highly educated, and those in all kinds of businesses. We were being watched and followed, and when the opportunity came, one by one Tutsis disappeared, being kidnapped and clandestinely murdered.

Rwaza/Ruhengeri, 1986

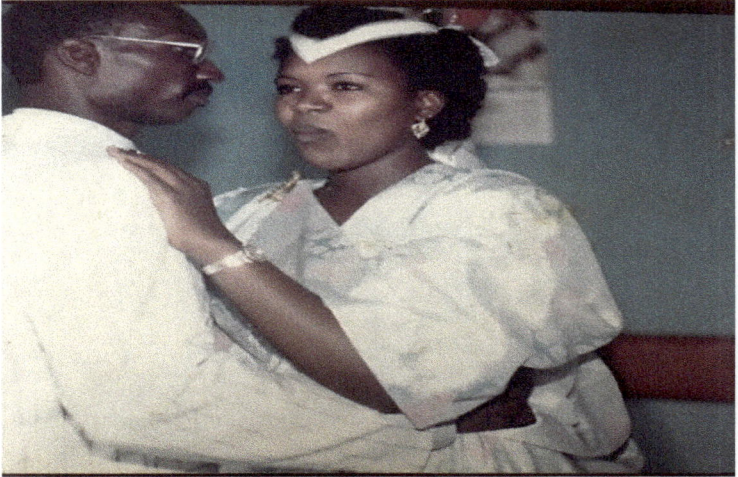

Wedding Day, 1988

The government would falsely accuse innocent, good citizens for impossible acts just to divide them and cause their neighbors to question their integrity. This way, people were cautious and suspicious toward each other. There was a private radio station that was spreading lies and hatred against the Tutsi tribe. My husband, being from the Congo, would ask me, "How do they know who is who? And who are those ones running in the streets with wooden made weapons?" These were just questions that any outsider would ask. I tried to explain these differences according to what I learned in history, but when he asked me, "So who are you?", the dynamic changed because I had to face the truth of who I really was. I was privileged to share my family story for the first time.

I was born in a polygamist family; my Father had two wives. We were eleven kids together: seven from my Mother and four from the other wife. Our Father married my Mother during the aftermath of the massacres of 1958, when the Belgians left the country, leaving behind the hatred that would mar the history of my country. By that time, the Hutu tribe took power; many Tutsi were killed, and the survivors were driven out of their land. Houses were burned down and their flocks were killed. My Father fled to the Congo with his first wife and kids, where he met my Mother who was also a refugee from the same cause. She had fled with her mother and young sister while her father and brothers fled in the opposite direction, ending up in Uganda.

Life as a refugee was hard. Grandma was worried for my Mother's life and safety. She was, at that time, turning seventeen. Grandma gave her to a married man who became my Father and she became a co-wife at a very young age. Father was challenged; taking care of two families in a strange country was so heavy on him, that he found a way to go back to Rwanda by purchasing a Hutu's identity. He became officially Hutu in order to go back to Rwanda. This is how we became half Hutus and half Tutsis. Father made his way back to Rwanda and settled his two families in Cyangugu, the province across the border with the Congo. We were all born there. He took a job at the local airport and made his way up to the "supervising" position. He was not rich, but was able to take care of us. Grandma told me that Father loved our Mother so much that it caused friction between the two wives. Father passed away in a car crash in the 1970's, and a few years later Mother followed him. We were left alone at the mercy of the world.

With my husband's questions, I went on trying

to establish the physical differences between the three tribes, which apparently didn't make any sense to him because it really doesn't. Then he said; "Let me guess. You are one of the good kind; I mean the nice ones, right?" I wanted so much to tell him than I am on the side of the weak ones, the ones destined to be slaughtered; that I am from the cursed tribe as they were singing. I wanted to tell him that we were scheduled to be killed like cockroaches, as they were bragging all over the country. There was no need to traumatize him beforehand, because he was about to live a nightmare.

I had never thought that with the suffering we had grown up with, that there would be more to it. I really thought that it was over; that I had made it out of the worst.

In January of 1994, my second daughter was born. The family was growing; life was getting better and better. We had made good friends and we lived in a good neighborhood. In our culture, when a baby is born, family and friends get together and come to welcome the newborn and to congratulate the mother. So, in early March, all my siblings, their spouses, and children came to my house. We invited friends and neighbors; we had food and drinks; we were having a good time and life was easy. There was laughter and jokes; the kids were playing; my family was very proud of how my life had turned out, and make no mistake, everything was working in our favor. Ahead of us, we wanted to see life as bright as the daylight. What we didn't know was that it was the last time we would see each other. It was our LAST SUPPER.

Graduation Day, 1993 in Kigali, Rwanda

The rumors had turned into tortures, the radio and newspapers were spreading hatred against us, and we were told that we were being watched. There was no escape; people were disappearing in incredible ways. We were marked "To Be Killed", an invisible mark on the forehead, you would think. In each Tutsi person's eyes, you would notice fear and sorrow, and a sense of helplessness. In every Hutu

person, you would see hatred and anger, and a superior attitude. They called out and shouted all kind of names: "cockroaches, snakes", humiliating words and provocations. There was not much to do or say but keep walking and thank God when one arrived safely at a destination. Some people were meeting for prayers and when caught, they were publicly killed or tortured by being accused of meeting and plotting clandestinely against the Government. It was a crime to be seen in pairs or in a group. Every night, we went to bed
not knowing if we would survive to see the next day.

Three weeks later, April the 6th, was a warm day, but very humid as usual. Evenings were quiet because we were under a curfew, but still neighbors were able to sneak out and stay together for a while. We were watching the soccer game on television; Zambia was playing that night. It was African Cup soccer season. Then, the power went off at the same time the horrible noise of the rocket was heard. The flames of the burning, giant airplane were seen from afar by the people who were outside. We waited for the power to come back, but it didn't. All the people who came to watch the game went to their homes not knowing what had already happened.

IKINANI (the Rwandan president surnamed himself meaning "everlasting or untouchable") was dead with all his crew. Among them was the Burundian President, who took a ride with the Rwandan President from the peace negotiations in Tanzania. Through the night, we heard gun shots and grenades being tossed. The killings had begun! The highly-positioned Tutsis were already killed. My sister, Laurence, and her family lived by the airport. They saw the Presidential plane going down and were terrified. They knew what happened in the very next minutes. She called me in the night and spoke to my husband. I was already asleep. Having a newborn baby, I slept when she slept and woke up when she did in order to allow my husband some hours of sleep too. So, he didn't bother to wake me up. I was awakened by the heavy noise of rockets; it was so loud, and so very nearby. Our very next door neighbors were killed.

My husband told me what had happened. I thought he had lost his mind or that it was some kind of joke. It was impossible for the president to die. He was untouchable! He told me again and I believed because for once I saw fear in his eyes. Our fate was sealed! Every once in a while, there was a grenade tossed, followed by gun shots; in between was dead silence! Even dogs didn't bark! Then, the tossing of grenades became more frequent and there were more and more gunshots. We heard screams and cries; we were in the midst of the some of the worst savagery in the history of Africa. Every Tutsi person was a suspect and a target of the Hutus. Poor or rich, young or old, we were all blamed for the death of the President. We spent days and nights hiding. We didn't know what was happening or who was killed. I still can feel it even today—the fear of death, the heavy atmosphere, the suspense, the heat in the back of my neck, the anguish, the smell of death in the air...the dark clouds in the sky, and heavy rain! Heaven was crying for the innocents' blood.

I was on maternity leave. My second daughter was born on January 08, 1994. She was turning three months old and I was getting ready to go back to school when it happened. I was still heavy with my maternity weight. I could not fit under the bed. My husband begged me to hide in the ceiling between the roof and the ceiling, but I was so heavy that I could have fallen and given myself away. As the killers were going house to house searching for cockroaches (Tutsi), I was fighting to keep my breath. I lived in fear every second. I couldn't cough or sneeze for fearing to give myself away. For ten days, I was confined in a hole behind the kitchen. Once in a while, I was taken out to go to breast feed my three-month-old baby; I would be rushed back into my hiding place before the killers woke up.

My gardener was one of them. He was a Hutu who worked for us for many years and we were good to him in many ways. He knew their agenda so he could let us know when it was safe to get out. I will always remember the day they came to kill me. I still can hear the gun shots in the ceiling and the shouts of the killer asking my husband, "Where is your wife; we know that she is a cockroach (Tutsi)." We spent days and nights hiding. We didn't know what was happening or who was killed.

They searched everywhere. My husband told them that another group came and took me. He persuaded them and then they left. In my hiding hole I froze, not from being in same position for so long, but also from fear. I heard them marching from room to room, beating up my husband and shooting in the roof and all the cabinets looking for me. I could feel every bone in my body freeze; every inch of my being was dying, little by little. I thought of what could have been done to avoid the chaos. Nothing came to mind except that we were born to the wrong parents in the wrong generation and into a weak tribe. Every day, I was dying, or at least, something in me was dying. My fingers and toes went numb--in fact I lost all my toe nails and a couple of finger nails—there was no blood circulation in my legs and arms from staying in one position for so long. From the moisture of the ground buried in the dirt, worms and other insects were crawling on my body. The pain was so intense because I was incapable of moving or scratching myself. I waited and felt all my body going numb. My brain was intact; I had time to think about things I had never thought of. I thought of how else I could have wanted to die, who could have attended my funeral, what they could have said, and now I was buried alive! By the time the war would be over, I would be long gone--dead at a young age. I thought of the pain my husband would endure raising two little girls if they made it out alive.

I refused to die! I made my mind up. So many people were dead; I was still alive and I had to fight to stay alive. Marilyn Ferguson wrote in *The Aquarian Conspiracy:* "At the level of ordinary consciousness, we deny pain and paradox. We doctor them with valium, dull them with alcohol, or distract them with television…Conflict, pain, tension, fear… these are transformations trying to happen. Once we confront them, the transformation process begins."

Yes, I had to confront my pain and the fear of dying young and unaccomplished. I had no possible way to ease my pain and my fear. I knew that if I made it out alive, I would never be the same. I kept my eyes shut, avoiding letting dirt enter them, so I didn't know if it was daytime or nighttime. I wouldn't sleep, fearing never to wake up and know the end of the story.

I trained my brain to see the bright future while the present was dark. I heard myself telling my story of how I survived! I must live to that day, I told myself. I thought of my girls and their children and that I was only twenty-three years old. I wondered where I would be in five years-- surely not in Rwanda! I hated the people and the politics. I wanted to go far away where no one would call me a cockroach, but where? I was still in the dark pit.

One night, my husband and my gardener came and took me inside. They had to carry me because I couldn't feel my arms and legs. The entire time I was in the hole, it was raining. The whole night the rain was falling; Heaven was crying over innocent deaths. We were afraid that the noise of the rain would keep us from hearing the killers coming; that they could surprise us and kill us. Leon told me that all of the Embassies were calling out their people for evacuation. The Congolese Embassy (he was from Congo) had set up a day and time for the evacuation. We sat there trying to figure out how to get me to the Embassy. Every thought we had was pointless. It was too risky to be seen with me because it was said on both radio stations that whosoever would be caught helping any Tutsi or hiding them would be killed as well as the cockroaches. We cried the whole night. It was hopeless. We were stuck in the midst of the killings. Leon was devastated; he even thought of killing himself rather than waiting to see how these merciless killers would kill me. I saw him losing hope; my hero was not able to protect me! He wasn't even able to make any decision. He had not many options, but even the two options he had, seemed hard for him to choose between—leaving me in the hole or trying to take me to the Congo. Then, I had to make a very hard decision. I knew that if I stayed in the hole, I might be there for many days. Maybe I could have even survived, but my husband and kids would end up killed since all expatriates were gone back to their countries. I knew that if I tried to get out and leave the country, I would be killed on the road, but my husband and kids would escape. Then, I convinced Leon that the best thing to do was to escape to the Congolese Embassy.

In few minutes, we were on the road. From my house to the Congolese Embassy the trip was about 15 minutes of driving, but it took us five hours to reach there; there were roadblocks at every one mile's distance to keep Tutsis from escaping their fates. Unfortunately, when we reached there, the buses were already gone; we were left behind to be killed. My fate was sealed.

The end was coming too fast. I was just beginning to live; it seemed like cutting a rose that was in the process of blooming.

We had to find a way to get to the Congo. I asked him to keep driving, following the main road to Congo. The trip from Kigali to Cyangugu (toward the border of the Congo) was normally five to seven hours. It took us two months to make it.

Living was beyond anything I could hope; death was a sentence well written on my forehead. I had grown accustomed to seeing death as a natural step of life; people grow old and die; others get ill and die, but this was beyond belief. It was a disaster!

Chapter Three—Hell on Earth

Like after the storm, the roads were filthy. All around were people's belongings. There was smoke everywhere; houses were burning and the smell of burning tires was stifling.

We drove our small, Jeep Suzuki, past dead bodies. The road was deserted, but about every ten miles were check points or road blocks. The killers were searching every car for cockroaches; they were shouting in victory over their found cockroaches—even the old, and young babies. They were happy in killing us. They had blood on their arms, on their hands, and on their chests. Their eyes were red from many nights of sleeplessness and drunkenness. There were many dead bodies all along the road. There were too many to be counted; they were piled up like firewood. There were also some people left half dead there who were slowly dying in agony, crying for help. There were babies left alive sitting beside their dead mothers. I wondered how long they would stay alive. Would the killers feel sorry for these innocent babies? Would they adopt them? Would they kill them or leave them and watch them die slowly?! There were women (Hutus) at every checkpoint.

Genocide in Rwanda, 1994

They were happy killing us!

They too were happy taking our belongings screaming, "Kill those bitches!" My head was spinning. I couldn't find a better way to die. I just wanted a short way and a death less painful. I wanted it well done, just quickly. I was in my early twenties and about to be killed. They were happy killing us! Their faces were thirsty for our blood; their eyes were red and angry and they had no mercy. There wasn't a good way to die, but they had choices in killing us. They were taking women to rape them and would kill them once they were satisfied. They had guns, knives, grenades and many other traditional weapons made out wood.

In Kigali (the capital city) and its surrounding areas, we were well known. Leon did the speaking and negotiating while I was melting in fear praying for divine intervention. Once in a while, we found someone who knew us, somebody we had once hired or someone we went to school with. They would plead for me, but once we went out of town, we were on our own. We reached another checkpoint; the search went on and they found me. I was taken out and away to be killed. There was no time to say bye to my husband. I was rushed, pushed and kicked. My knees were shaking and when I fell, they pulled my hair to get me up. They spat on my face in disgust. I remember every detail as if it was yesterday. I stood before my killers shaking like a leaf, my mouth dry and my throat paralyzed. I wanted to disappear or to melt miraculously rather than face those cruel men. It was raining. April is a rainy month in my country. It was so dark and cold that it seemed that even nature was sad about what was happening. The killers were screaming to each other; some were in the car dealing with my husband. It was then that he gave them the car keys; they took the car for my ransom. I was released to go but they said, "Let her go, she will not go through the next checkpoint."

I didn't eat for many days and was forced to breastfeed the baby, as otherwise she could cry and attract the killers' attention. At one point, she was too hungry; she sucked everything out of my body until I passed out. My husband had to ask if somebody had a fruit or anything to eat. He was given an avocado. We had no plates and no knives. I had to dig in it with my fingers and my mouth like a monkey. I had to be strong for my baby. Soon she couldn't find anything from my breast; she was hungry and weak and became sick with pneumonia. I couldn't keep her on my back so I had to carry her in my arms. Her little lungs were filled up. I was carrying her in my arms and

I was too weak, which slowed our journey. She was coughing and we were afraid that she would give me away. We walked through the night, avoiding the main roads and hiding in the day time. My husband was carrying our first daughter, who was four years old, and I was supposed to be strong enough to carry the baby, who was then three months old.

I began to feel her coming death. In my mind, I couldn't avoid the picture of her little dead body. There was no time to bury. Dead bodies were everywhere around; the thought of dogs fighting over her body was a torture. I felt cold sweat on my back and my womb was shaking. I didn't sleep. I spent days and nights holding her in my arms crying to God to heal her and at the same time waiting for her last breath to escape. I was tired and couldn't keep up with others and the baby was too sick to carry so we stopped in the province of Gitarama, waiting for her death. I prayed through the night that God would be merciful to us. Since death was imminent, couldn't it happen less painfully?

Soon the city was evacuated. They said that the rebel Tutsi were advancing. We didn't know what was going on. The military and militias were forcing people to flee along with them. We found ourselves hostages. The last bus came and they pushed everyone in and took off. This was their strategy to escape by taking hostages of all the weak and elderly people who didn't have ways to flee. The fear of being captured by the rebel Tutsi was so intense, they had no time to look at me. On the road, all military and militias left the bus, leaving their families on it, and gave orders to the driver to drive to province Cyangugu. This is where we were heading anyway.

We reached a place called Kivumu, in the province of Kibuye, at night fall. The search went on for an hour. This was the last checkpoint before reaching the final destination. Nobody of my kind escaped this place. I knew then that my time had come to an end. They took me and my four- year-old daughter out of the bus; we were lined up waiting to be killed. My husband and the baby were waiting with others for the bus to take off, leaving us to die. About five people were between us and the killers. I remembered that I had to say a final word to my husband. I went to him and thanked him for being good to me. I told him, "You don't have to watch how I will be killed, just flee for your life. When you reach your country, get a woman of your tribe who will raise the baby. Never go back to Rwanda. I am sorry for bringing you in this trouble." Before I could finish my last words, he screamed, and the leader of the group of killers came over. By talking to Leon, he discovered that he didn't know much of the Rwandan language, so he asked what was going on. In poor kinyarwanda, the language of Rwandans, my husband explained that they were going to kill his wife and daughter. He showed him our marriage certificate. The guy came back and told his crew how wrong it could be to kill me since I was legally married to a Congolese man, that the law granted me his citizenship automatically. He called me aside. I was terrified. I could feel my bones melting; my lips and mouth were dry; my throat was paralyzed and I was just staring at him. He asked a few questions. I don't remember any answer. One thing I do remember is that he took my four-year-old little girl and me back to the bus and the bus took off. I will never forget the people who were left there--the death in their eyes. One of them was an old woman who gave me an avocado when I passed out due to hunger. She was nice and clean. She was probably one of the few wealthy Tutsi who paid to be protected. Her daughter was taken to be a wife by one of the militias so to be protected. The entire journey we said nothing to each other; we were communicating heart to heart and with facial expressions, avoiding anything that could draw attention to us. When I was taken back to the bus, I looked back to her as if somehow, I needed her blessing. When we made eye contact, she nodded. Right in my heart I got the message, "Go on, Baby. If you make it, tell the story." Like a zombie, I embarked on the bus again. I was very skeletal and very weak. I was emotionally exhausted and physically spent.

We see God working miracles throughout the scriptures. Sometimes it sounds too miraculous to hope or think about its probability in today's life. I saw a non-educated village man spelling out loud the law and regulations concerning the marital law. Will you ask me what a miracle is? There were so many instances in my life when I knew without a shadow of a doubt that God's focus was on me. I am taking time to write those seemingly little things, just to help you realize that if the Most High God said that He watches over the little sparrows, you are more than a sparrow. So am I.

People talk about luck and coincidence; I don't believe I was lucky. I believe that I was graced!

That was my first introduction to "a compassionate and gracious God, slow to anger, abounding in love and faithfulness." Grace showed up in my life free of charge. I didn't deserve it. I didn't ask for it. I was resentful, wounded, and bound by anger and hatred. This is what grace is: "undeserved favor". Now that I yearn to make known what God has done in my life, trying in my poor and small ways to channel the gift of grace, help me out, my friend, and reflect on your life's journey. Find places where you thought, like me, " God where are you?" In an attitude of humility, ask the Holy Spirit to show you the work of Grace during those moments. You will see that He never stopped loving you; He always cared for you. I don't think that Paul (the Apostle) recognized grace the first time he prayed for God to deliver him from his thorn in his flesh, nor the second time, but through pain and suffering he grew to acknowledge that it was the grace of God that carried him through, making it possible to endure the thorn in his flesh.

Grace is everywhere. Look around; you will see grace. Grace reminds me that I am a sinner, but grace doesn't condemn me like a sinner. That's why it is GRACE! I saw grace on the road to Congo; I saw grace through the angry killers—blood thirsty, evil workers. Who am I to escape it? I am graced. I was sentenced to death in the same way we were all doomed to die in sin, but grace broke through in the form of a man,

Jesus Christ, hung on the cross as grace in action. So, you may ask then what about these who were killed? Why God didn't save all of them? My friend, I am not God to answer such a question, I would only help you understand what I wrote in the beginning of this section;

"To everything there is a season,

A time for every purpose under heaven:

A time to be born and a time to die…"

So, are you still wondering whether God is there or not? Someone asked me to explain grace concerning those who were killed so roughly. It sounded as if they just wanted to say that God is not fair. My answer is that God is not fair. God is just and faithful. He has put the law of nature in place and will make sure it is respected; everything has a beginning and an end. We are born and we will all die. When to die and how to die we do not know. The law of the strong and the weak is always in action in our midst; evil and good are also in every person. For us believers, we know that the physical death is nothing but an entrance to the eternal life, where death will have no power and where there will be no pain and suffering. Those who were killed roughly finished their journey. They reached the end of the road. They escaped so much that we, who survived, had to go through. It requires grace to understand that there is grace even in dying.

Dead bodies were all around!

understand th t ther is most . dwia

Don't

Chapter Four—The Longest Night

The bus drove away and stopped, for the night had fallen. The driver was tired and the road was not safe. He asked everybody to get off except for women with babies and the elderly. I stayed in the bus with a few others. We would resume the trip early in the morning. He told everybody aboard that he didn't want any killing on his bus, otherwise he would leave them and go back to Kigali. They pitched tents outside the bus and made fires with firewood. They drank and smoked. They spoke evilly about cockroaches. They swore to clean up the bus in order to reach their destiny, meaning they would kill my daughter and me. We paid some money to the driver to let us stay on the bus through the night fearing the anger of those bloodthirsty creatures. The night was long! This was my Gethsemane.

Though I had trained my mind to see the brightest future, at this point my mind was shifting back and forth. I tried to look for the light at the end of the tunnel, but all around me was pitch dark. My heart was racing. I could feel every drop of my blood rushing through my veins.

Every breath I took was as if it was my last. I was shivering. I had a high fever and it was as if all my body was on fire; my eyes were swelling and on fire as well. I had lost so much weight I was half of my original size. I couldn't remember the last time I had eaten.

I saw my reflection in the window of the bus. I didn't recognize the person staring at me. She seemed very old; her face was wrinkled and there were pouches under her eyes showing her misery. My lips were dry and surrounded by dried blood which made it difficult to open my mouth. I squeezed my baby as hard as possible, keeping her close to my body, just to support my shaking. I tried to shut my eyes but I couldn't because I thought it was a nightmare and I couldn't wake up from it. I tried to think of why I was there in the first place, but my mind was blank.

It must be a dream—a nightmare! I heard my heartbeat interfering with the bus driver's watches (he had six watches—three on each arm), then I knew I was awake. There was no nightmare. It was real. I was living my last minutes.

Across the seat, my husband and my first daughter were sleeping. He was holding her tightly. I gazed outside and saw the fire going to sleep too. Everybody was tired, the night was spent, and I was in midst of nowhere, alone in the world. I felt tears, hot tears, flowing on my boney cheeks causing my eyes to burn. The tears were salty and hot for I had long told myself that if I dared to cry, the spring in my head would never stop. I shut my eyes and told myself, "No, you can't do it." Those tears left a trace on my ashy cheeks. Every tic-tic of the driver's watches reminded me that I was alive and alone. How I hated being alive!

I hate being alone and will always hate it. Loneliness can be a result of many events in our lives: a divorce, a death of a loved one, imprisonment, a move to an unfamiliar place, whatever reason that causes loneliness, loneliness tears away our emotions and very often it brings a feeling of being isolated from the rest of the world.

Loneliness reminds you that you once lived, once had friends and family, and that now they are all gone, leaving only an inner pain and emptiness impossible to fill. It is also possible to feel lonely while in a crowd, the feeling of "No one knows I am here, no one cares, I am invisible," etc.

There was no moon, nor stars in the sky. It was pitch dark. My heart was heavy with sadness. I knew the pain of giving birth and I also knew the anguish of waiting to be killed, but I didn't know how it feels when the soul escapes the body. I was resisting my pain and loss and tried to avoid relating it to God. I have had many experiences of God being with me in my suffering in past years, but this time, I felt so abandoned that I didn't want any part of hearing about God and His love, because there was none around me. The facts were there before my eyes; God wasn't going to change events for me. I was supposed to sink or swim. I looked at my husband who was still sleeping and felt angry. How could he be sleeping while I was in pain? I remembered Jesus in the garden. An ache in my heart made me aware of His pain and agony when He asked his disciples, "Are you sleeping? Could you not watch with me one hour?" Matt 26:40.

This was my hour of agony. So many good people were killed while praying on their knees. Why pray? Then, I heard myself saying, "God, if it be possible, let this cup pass me, but not my will but yours be done."

My friend, if you are struggling with loneliness today, let me tell you one sure thing; you can rest assured that God doesn't desire for you to be lonely. He desires for you have friends, to be a friend, and moreover, he desires to have a relationship with you. You can ask Him to free you from loneliness and He will do it. Ask Him to be that friend who will not abandon you when the night grows dark, that friend who will not be ashamed of you. He, alone, will never pull away from a relationship. He will never give up on you. His love never runs dry; He always has enough to give. He loves your fellowship. In fact, He says to you and me, "Lean on me." When God is your number one friend, He becomes the source of your joy and happiness; you will find that you will always have more to give to others.

It takes time to build a friendship. Good friends don't show up on your front doorstep instantly. You will have to commit to building those friendships and you shouldn't take them for granted when you have found them. By training my mind to see a better tomorrow, during those lonely hours, I thought of writing a book when all the storm would be over. I even thought of how I would introduce it.

Then, the driver rose and interrupted my day dream. It was about four in the morning and we must keep on going. It felt as if it was an eternity. The night was too long. Every minute lasted forever, but eventually the morning broke and a new day began. Exhausted and hungry, I was too weak to get out of the bus, but the driver insisted that we all get out for a headcount. We went outside and soon everyone was lined up for a final checkup before resuming the trip.

The people on the bus were angry because they wanted me killed so badly that they didn't give me my seat back. I had to travel the rest of the trip standing by the door of the bus on the rough, rocky road to Cyangugu. How much I wanted to jump out and kill myself! I would count one, two, and by the time I counted three to jump out, something would just stop me somehow. During this longest night of my life, the painful feelings that accompanied my suffering were on all levels of my being: physical, emotional, mental, and spiritual. It has been proven that some other feelings may be experienced such as: shock, sadness, depression, and denial. We might have resentment and self-pity. There is often also a sense of being lost. We may feel that no one cares—not even God. There may also be pain in our bodies where there was never pain before: headaches, backaches, stomach aches and more. It is hard to go on believing and trying to live during times of torture.

The poet Kahlil Gibran says, "Pain is the breaking of the shell that encloses your understanding." No one will better explain pain than one who has experienced it. Amazingly, I didn't feel any hatred against these people, instead, I felt so curious wanting to know what was going on in their minds, if they had any. I wanted to know what kind of fiber their hearts were made of; did they have the same blood running in their veins as in mine, and frankly, I felt sad and sorry at the same time for them. They were not my enemies because they didn't know me. I saw them as robots programmed to kill. They had no life and will, but I was in great pain because of them!

C. S. Lewis called pain "God's megaphone." He lost his wife to cancer. In the midst of his pain, he said that to him it seemed that God was not listening, as if a door was slammed in his face, "and all that I could hear was the sound of bolting and double bolting." Lewis was a brilliant writer and lecturer, but his own taste of suffering changed his style forever. He said that, rather than being evidence that God does not care, pain is overwhelming evidence that He does. This kind of experience changes the way we approach suffering and pain. It prompts us to have compassion and grace once we are over the valley. God uses our growth out of pain to make us more effective in our faith. It brings us to a higher point of service. It conforms us into the likeness of Jesus Christ, so that we will become the people He can use.

This experience of pain and suffering has helped me so much in my daily walk, as I meet different people undergoing pain in different ways in my work as a chaplain. I am not saying that God allowed me to go through hell to train me on how to become a good chaplain, because He has many ways to train and shape us, but this season of my life has softened my heart. Tenderly, I can look in the eyes of a suffering person and without words I understand their frustration, confusion, and even their anger toward God.

George Wald, (the Nobel Prize winner), says; "When you have not experienced pain, it is rather hard to experience joy." Right! There can't be a resurrection without death, and no one is healed if they were not sick in the beginning. Today, I look back to that night with gratitude to God who sustained me. I am able to narrate the anguish I felt, not so that you will feel sorry for me, but to encourage the one who is going through the dark days or nights of their lives.

I want you to know that it's o. k. to be angry, that hatred or confusion during those dark moments is natural, but don't dwell there. It is dark and it may even stink; it may be cold or burning; you don't see your next step—just BE yourself! Be there and tomorrow you will still be you. Every step, every breath, every effort you make pushes you toward the end of the tunnel. You are *going through!* Please don't stand up in a "why me" attitude.

There is a country song that I like so much. It says that, *"If you are going through hell, keep on going. Don't look back, don't show your fear, keep on moving, 'cause you might get out before the devil even knows you were there."*

This very book was born in my soul during that longest night of my life. I refused to give up. I refused to sleep for fear of not waking up again. I knew that there must be a reason I was living that night. I am so thankful that I stayed awake. I was granted a measure of strength I can't tell about because I don't understand all the facts, but I know it must be a gift from heaven. Back then, I didn't know what I know today about God (I don't claim to know much about the Divine and Mighty God though).

One of the definitions of "grace" is *undeserved favor*. There was no trace of grace when I was being tortured, there was no love of God in the eyes of the killers, and there were no angels singing to remind me of heaven. There were bullets flying all around and machetes being sharpened, but now, when I look back to my journey, I see grace at work. I see the invisible hand of God intervening on my behalf. I wish I could tell you that my faith carried me, but it would be a good lie.

This is how incapable I am when I am asked, "How did you then escape?" My answer is my definition of "Grace". I just kept going, moving from nowhere to nowhere. I really don't know what happened because I was supposed to die, but I am alive today.

I may not know where you are in your nightmare. I may not feel exactly your pain. I want to encourage you that if you die during your fight to stay up, please die like a hero, and if you make it through, be an expert and help someone else to understand pain and anguish. Remember, "*Sorrow may endure for a night, but joy comes in the morning." Psalms 30:5b*

Though life is not fair, God is faithful. You might be angry about this statement and it's o. k. It doesn't make sense when life hurts, when experiencing injustice, when it's dark and no one understands, but trust me on this, at the end of the tunnel when you look back, it will make sense. I don't claim to have figured out all the whys I had to go through what I went through, nor have I found answers to how so much evil can spread in a fraction of time and claim innocent lives as it did in my country, but when I studied the life of a man called Joseph, the one sold by his brothers, I tried to think of other ways he could have passed through to get to his prominent position in the Egyptian government. He surely was not going to get there by sending in his job application on line. In fact, there was no job offer for "Pharaoh's house manager" even if there could have been an advertisement in the newspapers. This kind of position is very key (priority to a citizen). Frankly, I can't find any other way he could reach there except through troubles and hardship.

When I crossed over to the Congolese ground, I wished I could pitch a tent there so I could keep my eye on my country. I loved my native country; it was difficult to let it go, leaving behind everything I had ever known, but one season was ending, and another was to start soon. T. S. Eliot said, "What we call the beginning is often the end, and to make an end is to make a beginning. The end is where we start from." The night was over and a new day was beginning. I knew that my life was transformed and nothing would be the same. It is a relief to end a nightmare; it feels good to wake up and shake it off and say, "I am glad it was a dream!", but in my case, it was not a dream, it was a reality. I was wide-awake. Soon, I was to learn another language. Things were going to change for better or worse. Change was inevitable.

Many of us do not handle endings well, because endings symbolize loss in some cases and grief is a normal response to every loss. We avoid dealing with grief and try to jump into new beginnings as if there was nothing prior to stepping into the now. Grief is a painful emotion, and we instinctively try to shield ourselves from this pain. As a result, we live in denial and carry a reservoir of grief from our previous losses in life. We fear endings because endings separate us from what is the familiar life. The separation can be external, which symbolizes the internal separation that is taking place. The external separation is often temporal, but the internal separation is permanent--otherwise it would not be an end.   Anytime we see the end as a loss or an absolute finality, rather than the beginning, we must remember that life is a cycle of many beginnings and ends. As long as we are living under the heavens, there will be new beginnings and ends for everything. Friend, if you can accept endings as part of a great adventure of the life process, you will increase your ability to live, love, and enjoy life.

We must reach the end of ourselves in order for God to do His work, in and through us.

Chapter Five—On the Other Side of the Lake

The lake, "Kivu," is the natural limit between Rwanda and Bukavu (Congo, The Democratic Republic of Congo). We share the same climate, and have had good relationships, especially in business. Life is always busy on the border with people going back and forth exchanging currency and buying or selling goods. During this season, however, Congolese people were afraid to cross over to Rwanda because of the killing that was going on. They were watching in shock and fishing out people who were thrown in the lake half dead. Some people were rescued this way.

We made it to Congo and were admitted to the hospital—my baby and me. I was running a fever, I had infections, and I was wounded in the head. Because of the lack of any treatment, the wound became infected. Because of the fear and struggles, I had forgotten about it. I was lucky to have my head on my shoulders because many people lost theirs. There would always be an empty space in my life. No one and nothing would fill it.

My life in Congo started in chaos. The morning I woke up in the hospital was the real thing. For a long time, I forced myself to think that it was a dream, but this time I was well awake. It was a new day; I was alive. I knew it because of the language spoken all around me; they spoke Swahili and were loud. My thoughts were slow and labored. They said that I was running a fever, but every part of my body was shivering. I had slept for good, long hours. I watched those strangers watching me, but I couldn't understand much of what they were saying. I couldn't remember who I was or why I was there. I was awake and afraid. I went to use the bathroom and perceived my reflection through the window. I couldn't believe what I saw! The image I saw made me dizzy. I was skinny, pale, and bald—they had shaved my head to treat my infected wounds. I was unrecognizable.

After a few days in the hospital, it became clear that a new adventure had begun. I had to face my fears; I was a stranger in a strange land. All my dreams were dead. My beauty and pride was washed away and replaced by vulnerability and self-pity. The pain in my head and the aches in my body made me forget almost every morning where I was. I always thought that I was dead—still buried in the pit where I had been hiding in the back of my house. I wasn't eating much at all, and consequently, I was losing weight gradually.

The day came when my husband took me home to get better. The baby was doing great and had been taken home few days ahead of me. We lived with a few of my husband's family members. As time passed, I began to see that my new family was hostile to me and my girls. I was suddenly faced with my naked self, open for affirmations and rejections, hugs and pushes, smiles and tears, all dependent simply on how I was perceived at the moment. This experience was, and in many ways, is still, the most important experience of my life, because it forced me to discover my true identity. I was starting my life all over again, but this time, relationships, family members, connections and reputations could no longer be counted on.

Let me take you back to my childhood. I grew up speaking my native language, that is "Kinyarwanda," and in school I learned French, which became my second language. After my parents' death, we went to live with Grandma (Mom's mother). She had not much to offer us, but we survived by her love. She loved us and devoted herself to our care. She became our caregiver from then on. She kept us together as a family and taught us survivor's skills. We were taught to love and respect everyone. It was not polite to speak your mind. We were told to keep everything to ourselves. We were instructed never to cry at the hand of the person who was hurting us, never to show weakness, to smile even when it hurts, and to remember to be thankful in every situation.

This is how I made my first entrance into my husband's family—a dysfunctional family—hateful and divided in every possible way. I didn't know their culture nor their language. Some of them who came to visit us in Rwanda were shocked by the way we were living. We had created a small family in a European lifestyle. It was a dream life. I lived in my glory with all my family showering me with love and approval. I had a cook, a nanny, and a gardener. It was shocking to them to see a woman who didn't cook on a daily basis. I became a spectacle. The last time they saw me, I was a true beauty, full of life and lacking nothing. Here, I

72

was in shambles, like a skeleton, with a bald head, clothed in the colorless, tired piece I had fled in. If I was going to fit into that family, I was to stand up and do chores, making sure that my children got some food. There was no time to recover from my trauma. My husband was always gone early in the morning and came back late in the night. We had a very limited relationship. He didn't know what was going on in the daytime and they made sure he didn't know. With the language limitations, I didn't know much of what was being said. I learned to watch facial expressions and got some clues. I knew that I wasn't welcome, but couldn't understand the reasons why my so-called in-laws could mistreat me and my children—their own blood. Later on, I heard that my husband was supposed to marry someone from the same culture. I was a dishonor for giving birth to two girls, for not having a male child was an insult in the family.

Edward Weeks said that: "Living with fear and not being afraid is the final test of maturity."

I wasn't afraid. I was ready to do everything possible to protect my children.

With this family, I had always thought that if I just tried hard enough, I could make everything all right, but nothing seemed enough. With my husband, a wall was built between him and us as we saw him very little, and when he was there he looked at me strangely, as if with disgust. He always seemed angry with me for some reason. I was slowly losing my husband and I couldn't bear the pain of enduring the treatment I was getting from my in-laws. Every day, I hoped to receive news from home. Maybe someone was looking for me, I kept thinking. Maybe one day we will go back home and have our little life back. It was during this time that I learned the language of "Swahili." I learned it by watching faces and listening to the tone of voices. Believe me when I tell you that most of my first words were only abusive language because that is all that I was hearing. I was committed to confronting life with or without my husband. I couldn't change the way things were going. I was in no position to make rules about everyone, but I was in charge of my life and the lives of my children. When they used abusive language, I responded in my language too. I stood my ground; I refused to be intimidated. Soon my husband became abusive too, verbally and physically. I was humiliated before all people.

Every night had a different scenario. I was thrown outside in the night, and not having anywhere to go, I spent nights on the porch. They convinced my husband to divorce me because I was a dishonor to the family. He kept me by pity, not by love, because I was not in any shape to be loved. I thought of my family. They had all been supportive and proud of me. I was once loved. I encouraged myself in thinking that soon things would get better and we would go back home. I would find some survivors of my family and life would go on.

In a while, the Tutsi rebels won the war in Rwanda and drove out all the killers. The Hutu people had to flee to Congo. I saw them marching on the street of Bukavu. They fled the Tutsi rebels who took power, stopped the genocide, and established the current government in the middle of June, 1994. Seeing them again brought a mixture of emotions; fear, anger, and resentment. On the way to Congo, they killed, destroyed, and stole, so they crossed over with all kinds of things they had pillaged—cars, cows, motorcycles, beds, chairs, and so on. We even heard that they brought all the money that was in different banks so the Hutu power moved to Zaire. They camped in the city. They pitched tents in schools, churchyards, and in every public place and they made themselves at home. They gave materials and money to officials for bribes, so they were privileged.

The entire city was immobilized as these people made their glorious entrance. With the protection of "Operation Turquoise," a French assistance effort, whose role during that time was to protect civilians and escort them out of the war zone, the Hutu military and militia used the operation to get away Scott free.

Soon, the city of Bukavu was trashed and destroyed beyond explanation. There were human feces everywhere, and smoke and abandoned goods. There were discoveries of unidentified dead bodies in isolated places. Then fear fell over the whole city. During this chaotic time, a horrible epidemic of cholera claimed so many lives in different refugee camps in Zaire, that thousands among those who escaped the war, died of this evil epidemic. It was then that the United Nations established the UNHCR, Red Cross, World Food Program, CICR and many other not-for-profit organizations which made their way to Zaire and the neighboring cities and countries.

They created camps outside the city. They were asking refugees to volunteer themselves and go to live in the camps. Many did, and others who didn't were forced to go. They began picking up refugees on the street and sending them to different camps.

It was then that my husband got a job with the UNHCR. He became one of the agents who helped with evacuating the refugees and taking them to different camps. All the poor villagers were taken to camps and all the dignitaries and business men and all those who pillaged the country, were left in the city renting or buying houses. They carried on their lifestyles at the same time they were corrupting and bribing the hungry Zairean authorities with goods they took from Rwanda.

With my husband's job, our lives improved tremendously. We moved out, got our own place, put our girls into school, and I was able to go back to school, finishing my Bachelor's degree in administration and business management.

Life was so good again. This season of my life brought me to dream and hope again, but as I have learned in life, "To everything there is a season, a time for every purpose under heaven." Ecclesiastes 3:1

Rumors began to take place in every conversation. It was being said that the Tutsi government in Rwanda was organizing an attack to pursue and capture the members of the ex-Hutu government. It was also said that the Tutsi people who were born and lived in Zaire for centuries were helping the Rwandan Tutsi government.

I was one among the accused; the troubles began again. We were picked up one by one and taken for interrogations, which meant long hours of humiliation followed by torturous behaviors. Soon, some people were missing. The struggles were real for the people of the Tutsi tribe and those who resembled us. Some wealthy people sent their families abroad and to the capital city of Kinshasa, but the simple citizens were falsely accused and tortured. I was pregnant with my third daughter.

While sorrow was killing me inside, there was drama in the family; their accusations, lies, and rejection were torturing me. Days were longer and filled with screams and strangers coming back and forth in the compound. My only place of refuge was the bed I shared with my two little girls; that was my home, my safe haven.

Any day I wasn't working in the kitchen, I was not allowed to enter the kitchen, meaning I had no share of food. I would be assigned to wash and clean stuff. I had never known that an empty stomach is like a blender churning; it hurt to be hungry.

I kept my head high through it all. I practiced the good manners my grandmother taught me. I smiled even when I was humiliated. I squeezed my eyes when tears wanted to betray me.

Someone said that, "Trials reveal our true nature." Yes, it is through fire that our character is developed. I knew some of my rights, such as the right to think, observe, and shut my mouth to the point where no one could make me talk when I didn't want to. I practiced these rights and they kept me alive and I still enjoy and treasure them.

I was accused of being a witch. I was made into a public spectacle in the compound. I tried to tell my husband that my life was in danger, but he asked me what I wanted him to do and dismissed it without any explanation. One day, one of his nephews humiliated me and slapped me in the face and pushed me, throwing me across the house, while everyone watched and laughed. By this time, my oldest daughter was six years old. She ran to me and hugged me crying, "Don't kill my mommy!" From that day on, she stuck with me. She didn't want to go playing. She followed me everywhere I went. I always pray that she will find room in her heart to forgive those people.

Speaking of drama, they had a meeting every night to report to my husband what I did and what I didn't do; she said..., she didn't greet..., she didn't cook enough food and so on.

They also brought empty bottles of alcohol and a so-called witness to prove to my husband that I was a drunken woman, just to add weight to my dishonoring their family. I sat there staring at my accusers without blinking or saying a word, waiting to hear what my dear husband would say in my favor. I had nothing to do with these individuals, but I had every right to seek protection from my husband. I asked him if he had ever seen me drinking, even in Rwanda. He spoke back to me in French and said, "I really don't know what to think anymore," and he walked away. I was left staring at an empty chair before my accusers. I wished the ground beneath could open and swallow me. My heart was beating as if it would escape through my mouth. My daughter sat there with me, holding my hand looking in my eyes as if telling me to say something to justify myself. I said nothing and they were laughing. Then everyone left the room just leaving me there. Knowing that all these people were strangers to us, my question was: what has happened to the man I married, the sweet and mindful guy I used to know? I learned that I couldn't control what other people do or think, but I could control my actions and how I reacted about what I saw or experienced.

Chapter Six—All Gone Without Saying Goodbye

Then, I got news about my family. My sisters were killed; their husbands and children nowhere to be found. They were presumed dead; they were all gone without saying goodbye. I was engulfed by sorrow. I was a castaway, remembering what a man had told me when I was begging for my life. "God is in heaven with His Son. You are doomed to die." I couldn't have agreed any more.

The memories of our last time together flashed through my mind, and a cramp gripped my heart. We had so much yet to learn and to share with one another; our time together had seemed all too short. It is strange how I still can remember the details of that afternoon. They were all gone without saying goodbye!

The painful truth of how hard it was to say goodbye started to root itself and take hold in my heart. I wondered if saying goodbye was going to ease my pain or if their just disappearing into thin air was better. There were no easy answers. Deep in my heart I longed to have said goodbye to my loved ones. It could bring closure to my pain. I had experienced so many forms of loss, and in most of the times I had no chance to look back or to say goodbyes. Each loss, each unsaid goodbye, created a deep hole in my soul. Eventually, I accepted the fact that life is unfair. I wondered if I could become a more whole human being because of the way that life had painfully destroyed my happiness and the fact that it seemed my deep desire to live a clean life was out of reach.

Loss will never be easy for me, but I am learning to let go. Goodbyes will always overwhelm me. I am working on how to reflect upon them instead of running from them.

I came to understand that goodbyes are as much a part of life as the seasons of the year. Through life, we gain and we lose; we find joy and we experience sorrow; we salute birth, and we curse dying. We celebrate weddings, we dread a divorce or separation, and the cycle continues through life.

The word, *"Goodbye,"* means "God-be-with-ye," or "Go with God." It is a very significant time for both the one going and the one staying. It gives strength and confidence that if God is with you through the journey, you will not fear or experience times of solitude. It is a blessing. I lacked all these benefits that come with goodbyes. I was an outcast! I was alone in the whole world, with no one to call, no one to talk to, and no one to share my pain.

My Sister Esperance with Aunt Musabe (RIP)

My two elder Sisters Esperance and Laurence
(RIP)

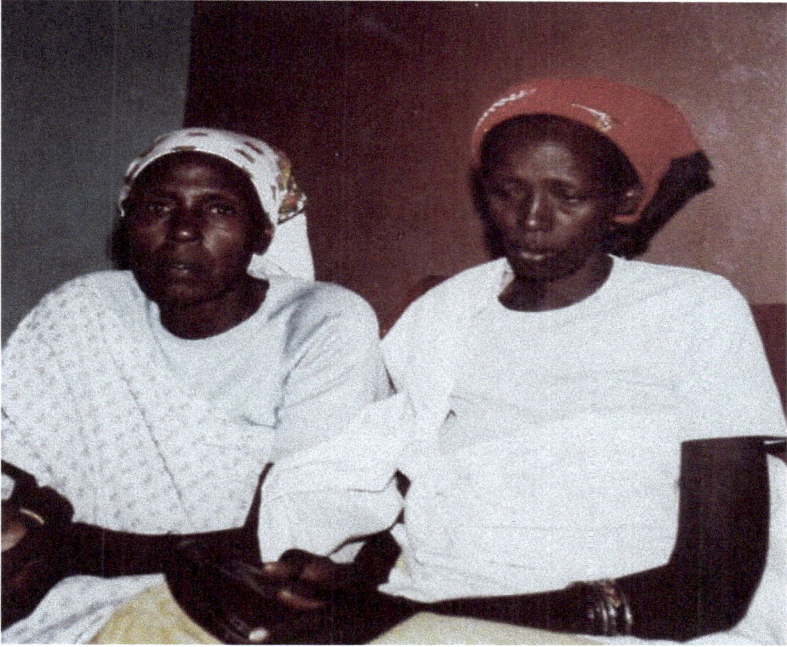

My Grandmother Madeline and her best friend
Bernadette (RIP)

Chapter Seven—Not Without My Daughters

Many women left their families and went back to Rwanda hoping that they would return to Zaire once things calmed down. Some fled to the capital city of Zaire in Kinshasa. I had nowhere to go. I was advised to go back to Rwanda by myself before the worst could happen, but I was supposed to go alone, leaving my girls because they were born of a Congolese father. I refused to go anywhere. I waited. I was taken into custody back and forth. I was tortured and accused of hiding Tutsi militias from Rwanda and their weapons. When I was released from the jail, I would be rushed to the hospital because I was pregnant and with all the beatings, I was in constant pain and at a high risk of losing the baby. My in-laws didn't know that I was pregnant and thought that I was faking being sick so I could get my husband's attention. My husband knew about the pregnancy and worked hard hoping to get a place for us before the third baby's arrival, which angered his family very much. He advised me to cross over to Rwanda and stay not far from the border and wait to see how things would turn out.

I knew that if I ever left my children I would never see them again. I refused unless I could take them with me. Otherwise, I would die here. For a long time, I told myself that I couldn't trust anyone. I had nothing except my two daughters. How could I leave them behind? With whom would they grow up and what would I become without them? There were so many questions in my mind without answers.

The authorities always came to get me when my husband was not home, which meant it took many hours for him to know that I was taken to jail. The last time they took me I thought I was going to die and I wished I could die. My pregnancy was advancing. I was nauseous; I threw up all the way to the police station. I met an old lady who was our neighbor. When she saw me, she stood up and began screaming at the people who were pulling and pushing me. She shamed them asking them if they had ever been born of a woman or had wives. She asked them, "Don't you see that this young woman is pregnant?" She knew me. We lived in the same neighborhood and she told them my story and how I was being set up by my in-laws. She was shouting, "Jesus, this is stupid! These idiots are heartless! Lord, have mercy on this young woman…" She followed and said that she would not leave until they let me go. She kept telling my story. Many other women joined her and followed. At the police station, these women told the police that I had nothing to do with Rwanda, that I had lost everyone in my family, or otherwise I could have left and gone back rather than endure all the abuse I was getting from my in-laws. I was released and I swore that that was the last time I would let a human being touch me or hurt me. I came to know that some of my husband's nieces and nephews were behind all these arrests.

I planned to escape. I took my two little girls as if we were going to have a walk, and I stole some money from my husband. I took off. I was filling out some immigration papers in the office when I heard a familiar voice outside. It was my husband coming to do some business, so I was caught in action and taken back home. I begged him to let me go because there was nothing left between him and me. He promised me that things would get better soon. The fear of losing my husband was so great that I was willing to do anything to get him back. Maybe, if I should have a baby boy, things could change. If I could work more, or if I gained some weight, I could gain my husband back or get approval in the culture. I was always teased because of my weight. These things I knew I could do, so I went to work on these three things.

I was pregnant and worked hard. I was sure that I was having a boy because that was my desire day and night. Things didn't change a bit; I was committed to working things out with everyone for my own peace. I did everything that was required of me; I did laundry, cleaned, and cooked. "If only I can do more, maybe I could be accepted," I thought. I was abused beyond explanation. I knew that I was where I was supposed to be. My condition was deplorable, but I knew with certainty that it was wise to stay and wait. I was afraid to look in the mirror because I couldn't recognize myself. I lost my pride and dignity. *Nietzche* said, "The one who has a "why" to live can bear with almost any "how." For the lives of my two little girls and my marriage, I had a "why" to live for. Besides, I had nowhere to go. I had no money, no friends, and no family.

Where would I start to explain to you the feelings I had in those moments, as I realized that someone was determined to destroy me at this point? From the day I left my home country, there was a seed planted in my heart because of what I experienced on the road to safety—the seed of "hatred." It had grown and filled my heart to the point of exploding. Every day, I felt as if the size of my heart was stretched, as if a heavy weight had been laid on my chest and pushed me down.

With my two daughters and a pregnancy
Bukavu/CONGO, 1996
A few weeks before the suicidal attempt.

Right after the suicidal attempt, May, 1996.

I was sinking in a deep sea. I was getting weaker and weaker every day. There was no need to fight anymore. I had failed. Now, it was my turn to live in my fear. The walls of my world were shrinking. Soon they would crush me and smash me. I decided to stay in the room all day and night, not because I liked it, but because the weakness in my body was growing. I lost interest in everything. I just wanted to slip away—to never see another day again. My days were long and my nights were filled with nightmares. I was haunted in my dreams. I was visited by my dead relatives in dreams; I spoke to them as if they were real. I was losing my mind and this was troubling and scary. There was no way out. I was going down fast and no one seemed to notice.

I constructed a strong mansion, built out of anger and hatred, and lived in it as a prisoner. I hated them and was angry at everyone, including God. How could a loving God be so cruel to me; what did I do to deserve all that had happened to me? Until when? How much can a person endure before God's intervention? Is there any such thing as God? I responded to my fear with anger—silent anger—and I hid myself behind it. Whether we are in crisis or not, we all tend to feel angry when we think we are treated unfairly. We have an ache for justice and we protest against injustice being done to us.

Anger is like fire; it can be destructive or it can be useful. When something bad happens to you—something you don't deserve—it is natural to get angry about it and that is not necessarily wrong. You might get angry with the person who has caused your discomfort, the world that allowed it to happen, yourself for not avoiding it, or God for not preventing it from happening to you. I tried to see other options if there were any remaining, and found one; I thought of killing myself. That way, I would no longer be a burden to my husband and a danger to my children. I knew that after my death, my children would blend into the family.

For many months, I rehearsed the plan in my mind. I even attended my own funeral. When I got every detail in place, I began detaching myself from my girls. I got up and made peace with the ladies of the house; after all, they would take care of my children after my death. I read the Bible, trying to find answers, but everything was so confusing and made no sense to me. With pain and disappointment, I asked: "God where are you? Are you so cruel at this point? Have you seen everything I went through? Do you even care?" I spoke boldly and for the first time I felt open to say what I had on my heart. I poured my heart out, like Hannah in 1 Samuel 1:15. I spoke for hours through that last night, the night before I planned to kill myself. I had kept silent long enough. It would be a double death to die with a heavy heart.

I went outside that night and looked up. To my amazement, the moon was high and bright. I cried until there were no tears left in my head. It felt so good to cry, since I hadn't done it for so long. I was twenty-three years old and ready to end my life. I recounted all my life to God. I looked at the moon and said: "Surely, You are powerful. You, who hung the moon up there with no strings to hold it, why would You make a beautiful thing such as the moon and put it over a rotten world? Do You care more about the world than people like me? A couple of months ago, I was afraid of sleeping because I might not wake up, but now I want to sleep and never wake up. I am so exhausted. I am alone and lost."

The night went on like this. I spoke of everything that was heavy on my heart. Between my speeches, I listened to the wind and the cold of the night. The crickets were singing their songs and frogs in the distance were competing. How much I envied those poor creatures! They were free to live their lives; they had a place to call their own; their lives were in order; they could sleep in the day time and awake to sing in the night. That night, I sat alone weighing the emptiness in my heart, lost in the noise of the night, suffocating my cry. I felt so helpless when I heard my own voice in the cool of the night.

"I can't take it anymore!
My burden is too heavy to carry,
 I am lost in the dark,
 I am empty and dry,
 I have no strength to cry,
 My heart is too heavy to lift,
Death has its power over me
Who will deliver me?"

In those days my husband was working with a UN agency settling refugees in the camps. He was gone for days so he never knew what was going on at home. In the morning, I took care of my oldest daughter and sent her to school as usual. She was six years old. I told her how much I loved her and wanted her to be a good girl. I told her to always love her sister no matter what. She is all that you have. She asked, "But I have you too?"

"Yes, Baby, you will always have me. Now you have to be nice to the family members. They are your family, and remember your dad loves you so much and will do anything for you."

She asked: "Why are you crying Mommy, did someone hurt you again?"

"Oh no, Baby. I am not crying and nobody will ever hurt me anymore."

I gave a good bath to my second daughter, taking my time knowing that those were my last gestures. She was two and a half years old. I was happy for her because she would never miss me. She would forget me in a few days, but it hurt to think of leaving my oldest. I knew it wasn't fair to her. She had seen too much in her short life. She didn't deserve living with the memory of a mother who killed herself, leaving her with strangers. I cried again until my head was hurting. I held her closely to me and smelled her body. I kissed her so much with tears flowing down my cheeks. I whispered to her the same things I had told her sister, and then I left.

Every step weighed heavily. I walked slowly and kept looking back as if I wanted someone to notice me and maybe stop me from committing suicide. It was painful. I didn't want to do it, but I was so sure that it was my only option. I was deceived and blinded by the pain and sorrow I had dismissed for so long; the effects of exhaustion were taking a toll on me. I was deeply depressed and no one saw it coming. There was no one to help me.

I had passed denial. Everything was real, and I was living in hell. Anger had only worsened my situation. There was no hope for me. I was depressed. Depression saps your energy; it clogs your thinking. You don't want to get up in the morning; you don't want to do anything. If you have any addictive tendencies, you are especially vulnerable to them at this moment as you are reaching out to anything that can fill the emptiness inside. This is a time when you need close friends—those who can stay and stick with you during your miserable and vulnerable times.

There are so many other emotions that can rise from crisis and people are different. Some people feel confused during a crisis, others feel betrayed by those who have hurt them; some feel afraid about the future, wondering if they will ever get through it, and others feel ashamed of the problems they are going through. I tried to fight to keep my head up and I lost the battle. I had reached the end of myself.

The enemy was at work to destroy what was left of me. My heartaches, afflictions, and trials stemmed from external causes first, and affected my internal life. The pain was real in many areas of my being. I was not aware of the damage being done inside; I only knew what I saw and experienced. When we are not willing to deal with the painful experiences that life brings our way, the pain becomes a "burden and a wound" of the heart. Afflictions turn into damaged feelings; hurts turn into habitual patterns of behavior that are destructive; failures and rejection turn into blaming it all on the world and on God. Then, we become slaves and prisoners. It keeps us from experiencing the fullness of freedom and purpose that the Lord has for us.

I was on the way to destruction. I walked slowly toward the lake. There was no going back; no one would miss me. I was a failure; unloved and unwanted everywhere I went.

I sat there staring at the waves. The lake was agitated. It was windy. I saw a branch and lot of leaves floating over the angry lake. A thought crossed my mind. "This branch was once a blooming beauty, full of life and admired by travelers. What happened to it and all the dry leaves that were once green and healthy? It must have been painful to be detached. They were doomed too. Nothing could absolutely bring back the life of that branch and put it into those dry leaves." This thought reminded me of my condition. I was cut off, I was doomed, and I was an outcast.

I tried to think of the goodness God had shown

to me in the past, but everything seemed unreal. "It was pure luck or a coincidence," I heard myself whispering. My head was spinning and my eyes and ears were on fire. I felt as if there was a fire burning inside my bones. The thought of leaving my girls made my stomach groan. I had forgotten that I was pregnant and didn't want to think about it. Yes, I had made my mind up that I must die for the girls to live a clean life. Their father would get another wife for himself and no one would ever remember me. The girls would get over it soon. "God is in heaven with His Son. You are doomed." The voice of the man who once wanted to kill me sounded real and fresh in my mind. This thought empowered me; I felt the power of hatred toward God and every creature and myself.

Then, I wrote down my name and address and a note: "Dear God, I don't know if there is such a being as God, but if there is, I will see you soon and will have a talk." I put it in my jacket. With satisfaction, I closed my casket and jumped in the lake.

From the day I left my home country, to the day I attempted suicide, I had been under an influence. I was drunk with hatred. I lived by its power. I hung on it and kept it as a precious pearl. I meditated day and night on what had been done to me; I revived my memories of the worst scenarios during my journey. "Sorrow, like darkness, like rain, blurs all borders and everything comes flooding in..." said Neil Graham. It is impossible to explain my anger without looking at the issue of trauma that I endured for such a long time. We must understand the power personal trauma has to shock and wound a person to the core. After trauma, most survivors admit that something has changed in their being. Traumatic events can create in us a hostile, mistrustful attitude toward life and the world. I made a critical conclusion that nothing good would ever come my way. My life was in upheaval and I could not find something or someone that would deliver me from my troubles.

Hatred is like a heavy blanket wrapped around your being, but still, it cannot keep you warm. It cracks your heart and every good thing leaks out. Hateful eyes see darkness and coldness; everything stinks; nothing is ever good. The sun never shines in the country of hate.

"You will never know the sweetness of Christ
Until you know the bitterness of trials.
You cannot know His fullness
Until you see your emptiness."

Charles H. Spurgeon

My consciousness was revived by a foul smell of a strange place. There was a terrible odor of decomposition. I felt heavier while lying down and soon found out that I couldn't move, as I was tied up to the bed and had a weight pressing on my stomach. It turned out to be warm compression to revive the baby in my womb. At least they figured out that I was pregnant. I knew that I had missed death. I was not in heaven and surely not in hell because I was cold to my bones. There was snoring and sighs in the room. I tried to open my eyes to see where I was, but it was as if they were glued and my mouth was dry. My jaw was numb and the back of my throat was on fire. Right as I was figuring out what was going on, I heard a scream just about three beds down on the left side of mine. This screaming and groaning said, "I am dead. Oh, God help me! I am dying...." Obviously, I was not dead, yet I was among the dying. Then I knew I had missed; the plan to kill myself had failed. I decided to play unconscious as long as I could. I didn't want to face the truth. Had the baby died? (Having both my arms restrained to the bed, I had no way to feel my womb. "What have I done!?") Warm tears flowed from my glued eyes and I heard a woman saying, "She is crying. Look! Tears are flowing. She must be in pain."

All around the room, people began talking about this woman who was found by the Nun's guards floating in the Lake. She looks like a Rwandan. They didn't know that I was pregnant. They thought that I had swallowed water when I was drowned in the lake. They said, "We almost killed the baby trying to revive her. Then, Father Andrè prompted everyone to stop pumping and we brought her here to find that she is pregnant."

They spoke in their language, which was Swahili, and by then I was able to understand it, for I learned that language in order to survive in Zaire. I came to know that in their culture when an individual attempts suicide, he or she will be brought to the community for punishment. They would beat the hell out of them so the individual would beg for his or her life, which is supposed to teach the individual to value the life they almost took away. Since I was pregnant, I escaped that spectacular beating. I escaped the physical punishment, but I underwent an emotional and mental breakdown following the botched suicide.

Chapter Eight—The Power of Hatred

I found myself in the hospital after the scandalous suicidal attempt. I had enough time to think and to look at myself, but this time it was different from how I had been looking at my life and my journey. I had to face my weakness and my wickedness. I was beaten in my spirit and ashamed of my actions. During those dark nights, when no one was there, I was given the opportunity to face myself and surrender my will to Christ. I saw how strong my will was—my selfishness, my pride, and the need to be in control of my life. I failed to kill myself and I couldn't save myself. I needed a real Savior, and this need was greater than the justice I so longed for. The anger and hate that were once my strength, left an unbearable emptiness in my life. I was no longer comfortable in my darkness; I longed for the light, the truth—something else that I had never experienced before.

St. John of the Cross in his book, *The Dark Night of the Soul,* describes his experience of being led by God to a place where the Lord lovingly "wounds" him. John of the Cross was arrested and imprisoned. He saw that God's divine plan leads us to a place where, through the pain and brokenness, we are ready to change and become more like Christ.

I had to come to a point of asking myself, "Did I make it this far on my own? If yes, I am a genius. If not, there must be God in heaven." Then why couldn't I save myself when I wanted to, and why didn't I die when I wanted to? I came to realize that if John of the Cross is true, I must surrender the tight hold that I had had on my life for so long. I reached the end of myself. There must be a beginning, but how do you come up from that deep pit?

"Come as you are," Billy Graham said. I stumbled in His love when the waves of the lake swept me.

> The Lord was there with me.
> He was in the waves.
> He it was who made the waters of the lake,
> He was there in power.

He commanded the waves to be gentle on
me.
He shut my mouth; not even a drop of water
I swallowed.
He quenched the roaring storms; they did
not over take me.
He valued my life, my useless life, as I
thought.
He was there; I felt His warm arms
cuddling me.
He carved a hiding place for me under the
raging lake,
All because He loves and cares for me.

I woke up in the hospital. I watched people
watching me. They said that I was in a coma—
wrong! I was well awake! Gradually, I started
opening myself again to the divine.

My third daughter was born with some
deformities, but with time, the Lord has healed
her. There is no mark or indication of that assault
of the enemy in her life. Here is why Isaiah
recorded the redeeming love of God;

"But now, thus says the Lord, who created
you, O Jacob (Brigitte)
And He who formed you, O Israel (put your
name if you want);
Fear not, for I have redeemed you;

I have called you by your name;
You are mine.
When you pass through the waters,
I will be with you;
And through the rivers, they will not overflow you.
When you walk through the fire, you shall not be burned
Nor shall the flame scorch you."

God in His mercy, out of a desire for a real relationship with us, will continue to allow us to fall flat on our faces until all we want is Him and Him alone. Because of His love for us, He is committed to do whatever it takes to free us from our selfish nature. The requirement is to acknowledge our selfish nature and let it go-- surrendering to His care. Surrendering to God means to embrace the change. In the surrendering process, change is inevitable, and no one has surrendered to Him and stayed the same.

I am still learning about letting go; I am not yet an expert. I have learned two important elements in letting go and will share these with you.

Letting go never seems to be easy, and there will not be any growth unless we can really let go. I have to keep learning this lesson over and over because I like to hold tight to everything which is mine, including my past and all the pain it brought. However, I came to understand that letting go doesn't mean that I give up or that I do not care. Rather, it means that I choose to use my energy in another way. I can give a new direction to my focus, choosing to focus on life-giving events, rather than digging in to those events that brought hurt into my life.

My friend, I do not know how deeply you have been hurt. I can't even imagine your pain; the degree of hurt is unique, but one thing I know is that each one of us will get hurt, for it is the law of nature. I wish that life could have been otherwise or things could be different, but wishing doesn't change the facts. Taking action does bring change. Listen to me well. Letting go does not mean that we ignore old ragged and bad feelings or dark memories. It does not mean that we have to delete the memories of our dead loved ones whom we miss so much. It means that when these memories come alive in our minds, we have the power to acknowledge them or to dismiss them and lock them out.

To let go is to allow something or someone to be left behind; it is to empty out, drop off, and unload what was keeping our load heavy, setting ourselves free from the weight. It is to receive freedom to continue leaving behind everything that had power to slow us down, to imprison us, to negatively influence our actions, feelings, and thinking. Letting go is a process; it is an attitude that grows within us. It is one step to our healing, however strange and unknown.

Sometimes, it is important to let go of someone. It may be through the death of a loved one, the ending of a longtime relationship, a daughter getting married, a child moving out to college, etc. None of these are very comfortable. Life will never be the same, but in letting go, we can choose to hold on to good memories and reject the bad ones.

Maybe you have come to realize that your expectations will never come to pass. What do you do then? Maybe your dreams and goals will never come true; what to do next? Maybe you have injuries; life left you injured in heart and body. You find it hard, almost impossible, to accept your weakness or your failure. It is hard to trust in the mercy of God and His forgiveness.

What to do then? Maybe you are being forced to leave the comfort of the place you dearly cherish—the house you grew up in, the school you attended, the company you invested in. You are being let go. You better let it go before it consumes you.

Most of us fear and resist letting it go, because this process involves change and change hurts. While being molded and fashioned, we lose the old image with which we were familiar. Change shatters the meaning and the understanding that we have created to make sense of our chaos. Every change is a type of death to an old way of living or being. The fear of not remaining the same is intense. I was consumed by the need for inner peace and rest, while at the same time I was afraid to lose the "me" I had become for so long. I was confused, disoriented, and lost. My life was filled with failure and shattered dreams. Hope was long gone; my inner poverty needed a touch of fullness, but I didn't know how to receive it. Robert Brumet said: "Change often shatters our sense of meaning and takes us into new territory where the old maps no longer work."

If every change is a type of death, then change is a characteristic of growth, and growth is a characteristic of life. Our fear of change is the fear of life itself. It requires courage to embrace change, to welcome the death of the old and endure the transformation to the new.

I dragged myself to my knees and cried out to God for change. "God, I stand before you with empty hands. I need you, Lord. Come and take over my life. I am afraid, Lord, afraid of the light. I am used to darkness, I am ashamed and alone. Help me to feel Your touch. Help me to trust that You will be there tomorrow when I will wake up. I am empty and tired of this life. I am exhausted. I can't carry on without You, Lord. I need an arm to hold on. Let You be."

The Psalmist put it together in a beautiful plea for help:

"My wounds are foul and festering, because of my foolishness.
I am troubled; I am bowed down greatly;
I go mourning all day long,
For my loins are full of inflammation,
And there is no soundness in my flesh.
I am feeble and severely broken;
I groan because of the turmoil of my heart.
My heart pants, my strength fails me;
As for the light of my eyes, it also has gone from me."

He made it very clear in the last verse of this 38th psalm when he uttered his vulnerability, and dependency on God;

"Do not forsake me, O Lord;
O my God, be not far from me
Make haste to help me,
O Lord, my salvation!"

While I was grateful for the lessons I was learning, and the peace of knowing that the storm had passed, I was afraid of facing the devastations of my past. I wondered what would become of my new life. I knew that things would not be easy. I was changing, but the world around me was to remain the same.

Makelele was an evangelist. He stood at the cross road every other day and shouted. He would read a scripture and sing a couple of songs and then pray for sinners. They called him "Makelele", meaning "noisy" in Swahili. We moved to a very busy street; there were so many noises with a mixture of cars, motorcycles, and people. This man positioned himself in the corner facing my front door, and day after day he came. I found myself interested in what he was saying, and expectantly waited for him to come. There was a kind of hunger in me—the kind of longing for something out of reach. Then one day I will forever remember, he came and did what he always did, and before the end he spoke words that pierced my heart;

"You whom I have taken from the ends of the earth, And called from its farthest regions, and said to you, you are my servant, I have chosen you and have not cast you away: Fear not for I am with you; be not dismayed for I am your God. I will strengthen you, yes, I will help you, I will uphold you with my righteous right hand." Isaiah 41:9-10

These words will always sound in my heart as long as I live. They brought goose bumps to my body and a quivering to my heart. I was shivering and tears streamed from my eyes for no apparent reason. I heard myself saying, "Lord, if this is You, You will have to confirm it to me one way or another."

In few minutes, I heard a knock at my door. When I responded, I saw that man at my door. He asked me to give him a cup of cold water. The fear of God fell on me. I was shaking like a leaf. He came in and thanked God for the cup of water, Then he said: "Today the Lord has answered your questions and He wants you to know that you are precious to Him. God will use you. Out of your brokenness will spring strength and healing for many people. He is God; that is His name."

He led me to Christ, and a few weeks later I was baptized. It was in 1995, and I still tremble when I think of that day and the strange messenger. He moved to the next city. I didn't see him again, but will always hear the sound of those words in my heart.

It is one thing to be saved, but it is another thing to walk in salvation. Here I am saying that salvation is the response to our saying, "Yes," to Jesus Christ to be our Lord and Savior, but this is not the end of the meaning. There is a walk after this. The journey begins, and the transforming process goes on day after day. We are advised to work out our salvation with fear and trembling, (Philippians 2:12) that we may become blameless and harmless, children of God without fault in the midst of a crooked, and perverse generation. (Philippians 2:15) I didn't know nor understand about this salvation stuff. Now that I know a little, I want to help to make your journey a little bit easier than mine was.

I had so many questions and I needed answers. I was not going to let anyone fool me, including God. If God is so good and all powerful, why did He let me go through hell. Why didn't He stop all that is evil? Does this sound familiar? Our world is filled with hatred and injustice. Every day we see innocent people mistreated and abused; the weak and the poor are ignored and trampled on. So, what is God up to? I came to learn that the heartaches, the pain, the dark seasons and the valley experience are not exclusive. It includes all of us. Saying, "Yes," to Jesus means that we are going to follow Him and this does not exclude us from these valley experiences.

Following Christ doesn't mean that we will

walk on a red carpet or fly when the road is crooked and the journey becomes rough. It means that the Lord will supply strength and wisdom to endure the journey and overcome the valley we are walking through. I can't describe the valley enough to convince anyone that it does not matter the depth of your troubles. I can't even find words sweet enough to comfort and ease your burden. I just want to remind you that nothing is to separate us from the love of God which is in Christ Jesus our Lord. My prayer is that you find strength and grace to carry on. I pray that the Lord will supply this strength and the wisdom needed to take you out of the valley in which you find yourself.

My prayer is that one day you will look back and say to yourself; it was rough, it was dark and hopeless, but I made it out! Praise the Lord! The reason I say this prayer is that I know it is hard, but you will make it. If I made it, anyone can make it, especially when you allow the Lord to be the leader. Do not be stubborn like a goat; try to be a sheep, just follow, the Shepherd knows the way out and he knows the best for you.

"Being confident of this very thing, that He who has begun a good work in you will complete it until the day of Jesus Christ." (Philippians 1:6)

Chapter Nine—Gathering My Broken Pieces

I heard a story told by Dr. Robert Schuller and was encouraged, because it speaks to the conditions I lived in a few years ago. If it can help you to understand your brokenness and how God cares about your being whole again, please do not delay handing the broken pieces of your life to Him who has the power to mend them.

He said that at the royal palace of Tehran in Iran, you can see one of the most beautiful mosaic works in the world. The ceilings and walls flash like diamonds in multifaceted reflections. Originally, when the palace was designed, the architect specified huge sheets of mirrors on the walls. When the first shipment arrived from Paris, they found to their horror that the mirrors were shattered. The contractor threw them in the trash and brought the sad news to the architect. Amazingly, the architect ordered all of the broken pieces collected, then smashed them into tiny pieces and glued them to the walls to become a mosaic of silvery, shining, mirrored bits of glass.

Dr. Robert Schuller concluded the story by saying: "Broken to become beautiful! It is possible to turn your scars into stars. It is possible to be better because of the brokenness. It is extremely rare to find in the great museums of the world objects of antiquity that are not broken. Indeed, some of the most precious pieces in the world are only fragments that remain—a hallowed reminder of a glorious past. Never underestimate God's power to repair and restore."

Yes, God spoke, but my life was still in shambles. I didn't know where to start. I was an infant learning to walk. I knew God was with me as He has said, but this was a theory. I needed more than the knowledge in the mind. Our lives will remain in shambles until we make Him Lord and Savior over our broken lives. The head knowledge is nothing but a theory, because even the devil knows that God is there. Through close communion with the Lord, we build an intimacy and the more intimate we get, the more He fills us up with His love. When we turn to the Lord, we are saying to Him, "I need you to fill this emptiness, this void, this loneliness in my life. I trust You to do it, for there is nobody else to whom I can turn. I am completely yours."

God in His faithfulness, will fill us with his peace and presence. He will also send good friends our way—people who will mentor us and help us to grow in God's ways.

After an encounter with Jesus, Saul (Paul) was sent to Ananias and at the same time God had spoken to Ananias concerning Saul's arrival and what to do with him. (Acts 9:10)

I needed good friends. A friend is someone to laugh with, someone to pray with, someone who really understands what I am going through, someone I can share secrets with, someone I can trust. The Lord in His faithfulness brought my way the ladies who once pleaded for me when I was being thrown in jail. They were mature Christians. They mentored me until my time to leave Congo. Someone said that, "Friends are wings when we can't fly." These women carried me. They taught me how to be a woman in the Congolese culture, and taught me the fear of God. With them, I spoke Swahili because they didn't know much French, so this way I perfected my Swahili.

In the art of mentoring, it is crucial to

understand that it is not at the moment that results are anticipated, but on the run down the road to life, when the mentored benefit from the lessons learned. Five, ten, fifteen years later, I am enjoying what I learned from these godly women. I felt so good when we were together, but life was different once I was alone.

I had gone so far down and so far away from God; it would be impossible to recover from my break down. I had no strength, humanly speaking, to come up from the valley; I knew for sure that I didn't have what it would take to stand up again. I shared my concerns with my elderly friends. With many prayers, I was reminded that it took days, weeks, and months to get me down the hill. It wasn't a one morning crash. In the same way, I would climb step by step toward the top again. I was advised to take it a day at a time.

Here are the names of my stairs: hatred, anger, betrayal, low self-esteem, distrust, emotional pain, rejection, resentment, doubt, and bitterness. You may be thinking that it easy to climb over hatred overnight, but, my friend, you haven't been down that stair. Anger, a small problem, you think! Well, I have been down those stairs and know how hard it has been to come up. I believe anyone who knows what I am talking about will agree with me; it requires

God's grace to climb each one of these stairs.

It felt so uncomfortable to give up my hatred, my anger, and other baggage because they were my force and my strength. They were my identity. It is impossible to take this journey alone; the need of friends is now or never.

Tough times are a part of life. We will all go through a lonesome valley at one point in our lives. It is easy to sing about God's goodness when we are upon the mountain. The sound of our voice is so beautiful and convincing, but it is so hard to believe that God is still good when we are in the deep and dark valley. Remember that the God on the mountain is still the God in valley. We do not need faith singing on the mountaintop. We need the faith to go through the valley.

> "One day at a time, sweet Jesus,
> That's all I am asking from you,
> Just give me the strength to do everyday
> What I have to do.
> Yesterday is gone, sweet Jesus,
> And tomorrow may never be mine,
> Lord help me today, show me the way
> One day at a time."
> *Kris Kristopherson and Bill Gather*

This song became my daily prayer from then on.

Maybe you are enduring deep affliction in your life today. If you are being tried and tested, remember the depth of God's faithfulness. You don't understand why; just believe in the strength and stability of God's affection for you. Take courage; keep your eyes on Christ. If you do not keep your courage, Satan will be too much for you and then you will give up. Let your spirit find strength in the Lord, who is your Savior.

I was still in the valley, surrounded by the mess of my past. The view of what surrounded me caused me to wonder if this Christian life was worth the pain I had gone through. There was no change on the outside. I was told that I became a new creature the moment I said, "Yes," to Christ. The remains of my old life were evidence of my brokenness. Like after an earthquake, I sat down in midst of the debris of what was my life. Broken, I asked the Lord to patch up my pieces. I just allowed the Lord to be the firm foundation of the new me.

Let me tell you something. Whether your life was leveled by the effects of suicide or betrayal and injustice, you have the option to rebuild your life differently and better. You can choose to address issues that are difficult to face, knowing that your life will be more stable following the process. You may need to piece your broken pieces together using special superglue; a sense of humor, or being an encourager to others in need. I can recommend to you the best superglue ever— the Blood of Jesus.

Many suicidal survivors surrender to a victim's way of thinking and tend to sleep away in their pain, but I chose to shake it off and rebuild my life and the lives of my children. It was not easy; the earthquake that ravaged my life was as real as a natural earthquake. Building on the same site made it harder.

People around me called me crazy. "She has lost her mind," they said. "She is now a born again," they laughed. "She met Jesus in the lake," they commented. Every time I thought my wounds were about to heal, there was a story told on me. Remember, I was being transformed from inside out, but the world around me was still the same.

My friend, I learned that admitting my anger and acknowledging my grief accompanied with prayer, was what brought me through my aftermath.

When I was a Chaplain (Clinical Pastoral Education Resident in the Pastoral Care Department) at Vanderbilt Medical Center in Nashville, Tennessee, I was called one evening to be at the bedside of a patient in the burn unit. I learned that burn patients undergo great physical trauma. The medical team explained to me that when a severe burn occurs, the nerves are burned as well as the skin. Because of the burning of the nerves and the destruction of nerve endings, it causes the patient not to feel the pain immediately after being burned. They feel the burn when the burn begins to heal. First and second degree burns will usually heal on their own, but third degree burns require the intervention of skin grafts. After a suicide attempt, emotional immunities are weakened as well, and survivors are more susceptible to the small things. As with a severe burn patient, a suicide survivor experiences an emotional third-degree burn. First is the shock and later the person will experience the crash of emotional pain.

The season to destroy was over. It was time to rebuild. It was the beginning of a new journey. I picked up the little strength left within me and went to the university to finish my studies. I ignored the grieving process, which is very important in the healing process. I had no knowledge and was rushing to move on. I will share more about my grief and the grieving process in the end. At this period of life, I knew with no doubt that if I was to make it, I would have to depend on God, not anyone else. I pulled myself together and little by little, I walked my way out.

With a Bachelor's degree in Administration and Business Management, I was committed to soar and climb any corporate ladder. My first job was to work with the new regime (Kabila's administration in the new Congo), the one that kicked Mubutu (Ex-president of Zaire) out. I was the secretary. They had no money; we were paid in food allowance portions. We were given a sack of sugar, a sack of rice, a sack of beans, a sack of peas, flour, a gallon of oil, etc. It was up to us to figure out what to do with it to get other needs met. Working with my elderly friends, I turned them into business women. Remember, a healthy friendship is a two-way relationship.

You cannot always be on the receiving end; you receive and you give away in one way or another. They were my spiritual mentors, but they were needy in other ways. I was happy to be a blessing to them in ways that changed their lives and the lives of many others in the community. We took small portions of the food allotment for our families and sold the remaining portions in the community. We made all kind of cakes. We made juices from fresh fruits. Even when I left the government work to work for Humanitarians, the ladies kept the business going.

There are stories told about those who have "died" and come back to life. We may not believe in those stories, but this is how I felt after this season. There are stories of the human heart that claim this same truth, people who felt that all the songs in their heart had died, that all the roads they knew were wiped out and they could go no farther. Then a kind of resurrection happened within them and they discovered "new melodies" and the wonder of "new roads."

They say that after the rain the sun shines. Not always, sometimes after the rain a cloudy atmosphere follows, but in my case the sun shone immediately. I could see my future bright as the day. I got hired to work for a humanitarian organization called, "Food for the Hungry International." I served on an administrative level managing funds and staff, including expatriates' staff. I reached the sky! I tasted the good life and my dream was coming true.

This time I was no longer called a snake or a cockroach. I was the respected "Mama Brigitte."

My life changed so fast that soon I was on a church leadership team. I led with my head, my knowledge, and many other skills, but my heart was not yet there. My social life was getting a little bit better, but my emotional and spiritual lives were still bound. I tried to fake my happiness and sure enough, I passed for a happy person. I became confused. Why was my life was still miserable after being told that all things become new? I was still dragging my old nature.

I didn't know that every valley has phases. I was still in a valley, only in a different stage—the "wilderness." I was beginning to see the light at the end of the tunnel, but I was not yet out. There was still so much to learn. At the Red Sea, the children of Israel saw the hand of God. They saw the delivering power of the most high God. He delivered them from Pharaoh; they crossed over and in the wilderness, they had one more enemy to conquer—their own stubborn nature.

I truly believe that God delivers us from our physical troubles to get our attention, but the real deliverance, which is the meaning of His involvement in our lives, is to set us free from our wicked nature (pride, the lack of satisfaction, murmuring and complaining, etc.)

For forty years, the children of Israel wandered in the wilderness, not because God had no land to give to them, but because they were not ready yet. He was not pleased with their heart's attitude, therefore, He led them in the wilderness to test them, to know what was in their hearts, and so He humbled them. (Deuteronomy 8:2-3)

The Lord is willing to set us free. His ultimate goal is to make us whole. Resisting this process knowingly or unknowingly, will result in some unhappiness or restlessness until we get it right; there is no shortcut to the wholeness. We must be willing to submit ourselves to God's will and time, otherwise we will abort the process and be good at nothing. Humility is learned through humbling situations—no other way.

Previously, I spoke about letting go of our pain and heartaches, but we must also be willing to let go of the good stuff God gives to us when it pleases Him to do so. We must be ready to walk away from the very things we once cried for; we must be willing to smell the roses along the roadside without clinging to the flower itself.

I became an example of restoration for many people, because some people think that having enough money means having it all in place. I tried to paralyze my pain to a point where it wouldn't grow. I kept down my anger and my fears, but I didn't deal with them thoroughly. It was as if I was putting a band aid on an infected wound, hoping to heal it. I had a double life; when I was with people in church or at work, I was one happy person—professional and very loving. I spoke of the love of God, restoration, never give up, etc., but when I was alone, I had to suffocate my cry in the night when no one was there because I felt so miserable and empty in my heart. I felt so powerless, I was incapable of taking hold of these truths for myself. I believed in everything I spoke about in the pulpit, but in my life, I felt little or nothing. Like physical pain, emotional or spiritual pain can be incapacitating. When your arm is broken, no matter how much you want to use it, no matter how important holding a can of soda might be to you, you cannot use that broken arm. A healing process must take place first. In the same way, emotional or spiritual pain can make it impossible to function properly if the healing process is ignored. No matter how much we want to trust again, no matter how much we want to move on with life, the pain simply doesn't allow it. Part of the healing of memories of the past is finding some positive legacy in the past itself; a story of survival. This doesn't mean that the evil that happened to us was a good thing. Suffering is never good in and of itself, but it is possible to draw from it strength and insight.

I lacked insight and had no courage to find the meaning in what I had been through. I wanted to move on with my life as if nothing had ever gone wrong.

When we reflect on the past with an attitude of

finding meaningful pieces, we can bring forth sensitivity, resilience, empathy, compassion, or courage, and this can lessen our despair about the impact the past had on us. We must be willing to clean our wounds and expose them to fresh air if we want to be healed. We cannot receive healing by ignoring or hiding the pain. A broken leg or an arm will cause more pain when we pretend that all is well and put weight on it, and the funny thing is that we may think that no one knows, but people get a glance at our behavior and wonder what's going on in our secretive lives. We need to be willing to acknowledge our own need for change and healing without turning this into self-destruction and self-hatred.

I lived in fear—fear of rejection or another betrayal—who knows what people can do again!

I was afraid to say what was on my heart, always hiding behind a smile. I won their approval because of my education, skill, and my social position, but still I had to watch out because this was the same community I had lived in, and these were the same people who had called me names and conspired and thrown me in jail—the same people who mocked me when I had nothing. I couldn't let my guard down; I kept an invisible separation (emotional and spiritual). I made friends though. When you have something to give, you will always have people around. So many people came around, it made me understand the difference between Rwandan people and Congolese people. Rwandan people do not reconcile so fast and so completely, but Congolese people are very quick to forgive and to receive forgiveness. One may say that they are naïve.

Overnight, I flew from the bottom of the pit to the summit of the hill, ignoring my stairs as I named them previously. I had so many responsibilities at work, as well as in the church and in my family. People counted on me so there was no way I was going to show my weakness. I was needed and important. If this sounds familiar, let me tell you what I learned from it. Hiding your pain will do nothing good but will make grief recovery more difficult. Do not let anyone silence you or tell you that you must get over it. No one lives your life. When all the lights are turned off, you will face your pain all alone. Climb your stairs one by one as you make your way up the hill. Do the same, but this time there is hope waiting over the staircase. It takes courage to be vulnerable, to be ourselves, and to cry sometimes. It takes faith to believe in friends and cry over their shoulders, but true friends will escort you and encourage you to visit your

With my Coworker Isabelle Claese
Bukavu/CONGO, 1996

painful places. You can't afford to go through this alone.

Let me tell you my mistake; I moved on with my life as if nothing had ever happened to me. I kept thinking that if I could make everyone approve of me, everything else would fall into place, as if the layers of my many years of pain and suffering would just melt. When I kept waking up in the midst of the night with fear and anger toward what happened to me, I knew then on that I was damaged beyond repair. I convinced myself that I could live with people without loving them. I could smile when I wanted to scream in anger—anything to avoid being myself. I somehow felt as if even God Himself could not be able to mend my brokenness.

So many people saw me as their friend, but none of them were my friend; I kept an invisible distance between the world and me. No one needed to know my life or my secrets. I was well educated with good manners from home and that was enough to fool everyone.

"He who formed your inward parts; he covered you in your mother's womb." (Psalms 139:13)

He knows your ups and downs. He sees everything that concerns you and wants you to live an abundant life.

Our memory of God's goodness is often crushed by pain. When we suffer sharp pain, or weary aches, or a high fever, we tend to forget the days of health and strength. We only remember the sharp intervals of weakness and sorrow. God's intention is to restore us, not to keep us in bondage. He wants you and me to live a victorious life, through which people around us will see Him and the complete work of His hands. He wants to heal you and make you an instrument of healing for others, however, there is a role to play in this process of healing and restoration. We must let go of whatever is binding us to the past. If we have a heavy burden on our heart, it will drag behind us and create a heavy atmosphere wherever we go. If there is a memory that takes away our integrity, or anger that steals away our peace, we will not be able to move on in freedom. It will always be there to stir up negative feelings in us, causing us to mistrust friends and causing so much harm in us and around our loved ones. We simply must come to a place in our lives where we agree to give up old insecurities which bind us, the painful memories which hurt us, and the lost dreams which discourage us. We must uncover those wounds which prevent us from feeling the warmth of love again. We must hand it to God to deal with it. We must lay it down at the cross. We must give God full control over our broken lives. This way He can start the process of healing--drawing a new blueprint of our lives according to His plan and purpose.

God cannot use a person who is not broken and completely surrendered to Him. We must be completely broken and fully emptied for this surrender to happen. We have to pour out our being for the Lord to start living through us. There must be a significant loss of the old nature in order to gain the new life in Christ. It was very difficult to understand that with all that I went through, there was a purpose for it. I believed that I was destroyed; that all that happened was to crush me and that it was luck to survive it all. At this point in my life, I knew I had made it out of the worst, but I didn't see any good or lesson out of my rough journey. I saw myself as another victim or one of the survivors.

I came to fully understand that there is a time for every purpose under the heaven—to everything there is a season. (Ecclesiastes 3:1) I was entering another season. There were seasons to kill, seasons to break down, a season to weep and mourn, a season to lose all in my past experience, and now the good Lord was taking me to another season—a season to heal, a season to build up, a season of joy and laughter, and a season for gain. There is no cheating in God's arrangement; there is no cohabitation between the old (my nature) and the new (God's nature). *"No one puts a piece of unshrunk cloth on an old garment; for the patch pulls away from the garment and the tear is made worse. Nor do they put new wine into old wineskins, or else the wineskins break, the wine is spilled, and wine skins are ruined, but they put new wine into new wineskins and both are preserved."* (Matthew 9:16-17) He made me very uncomfortable in the little financial breakthrough He gave to me to remind me that it wasn't over yet. In my own understanding, I thought that I was destroyed, damaged, and beyond repair.

The uneasiness in my heart, the lack of satisfaction, was just to teach me that only He can fill and satisfy a longing heart. Yes, I was broken, but not damaged. I was not crushed, for the purpose of the brokenness is not to destroy but to shape us into the figure that fits the purpose for which He made us. Trials, troubles, and tribulations help to develop and shape our character. I don't think that there is another mighty tool to build growth and godly character better than trials and tribulations. Trials reveal what we are depending upon. Trials take away the security and support in our lives. We have nowhere to turn; we have no other option but trusting God. "The testing of our faith develops perseverance. Perseverance must finish its work so that you may be mature and complete, not lacking anything." (James 1:2-3)

Also, trials force us to take what we know of God and apply it to real life situations. Trials provide the context for us to apply the truth of God's word in a practical way. I am not saying that God is behind every evil thing that happens in our lives. I am saying that He is the one who supplies all the strength to endure and is the one behind all the repair and restoration. It is not God who threw the three Hebrew boys into the furnace of fire, but He is certainly the one who gave them faith and courage to embrace the challenge. He did not sell Joseph into slavery in Egypt. His brothers did, but God was there with Joseph. He worked everything for the benefit of Joseph. (All things work together for good to those who love God and who are called according to His purpose.) In my despair, I thought that I was beyond repair. The damages were too great. The pieces of my broken life were scattered. It seemed impossible to put them together, but the Lord glued them together with His love.

It doesn't matter how far or how deep you have gone. It is not the number of your trials and tribulations that matter to God. It is your brokenness and surrendering attitude that invites God in. When you acknowledge the emptiness within, when you reach the end of yourself, when you are sick and tired of your own ways of living, then, it is time for the Lord to step in. When the fear of remaining the same is greater than death itself, then you are ready to embrace the new life in Christ Jesus.

While teaching the benefits of trials, my professor asked our audience how many would like to be admired and cherished like diamonds. Half of us raised our hands. He then asked how many would want to be like gold. Some raised their hands. No hand was raised when he asked how many would like to be like wooden jewelry. When he explained how much fire these stones must endure in the refinery to become what we all admire and lust for, it really came home to all of us that trials refine our character and transform us into the likeness of Christ, who for the joy that was set before Him endured the cross, despising the shame, and has sat down at the right hand of the throne of God. (Hebrews 12:2) See, there is a price for joy.

Trials will come your way. That's

natural. The question is, how will you respond to them? Will you let them destroy you or will you catch them one after another and master them, challenge them, and learn from them, being shaped and molded to the point where when God sees you, He sees the image of His Son reflected in you.

Trials are not to destroy us or damage us, but the way we respond to them determines how deep we are willing to be cleaned and refined in our character.

No one is immune to trials, because the trials that come in our lives vary from time to time. We never get used to them; we never know what comes next. Writing this topic does not make me an expert on the topic. I am just sharing the little experience I have gotten from the type of trials that were assigned to shape me. Am I done? Am I completely refined? The answer is NO.

I wish I was well done! However, we know that it is a journey. The process goes on as long as we live and are willing to be refined. If any of you is well done, well refined, please put the book down and teach us how you made it to perfection. I will forever be grateful for your teaching and accomplishments.

The word of God tells us that, *"But we all, with unveiled face, beholding as in a mirror the glory of the Lord, are being transformed into the same image from glory to glory, just as by the Spirit of the Lord."* (II Corinthians 3:18)

In 1998, when the political crisis took another toll in Congo, Kabila's government disassociated from the RPF (Rwandan Patriotic Front), and the eastern part of the country suffered again. The group Mai Mai (an old Congolese rebellion group), joined him and fought against everyone who was originally from Rwanda. My family became a target again. I am not a political expert. Please understand that these are not facts. I am just sharing the way I saw things—my own interpretation of the situation. We had to flee again, leaving everything we worked hard to build behind. I found myself in Kampala, Uganda, with three little girls and a pregnancy underway of the last child.

Another step and my journey continues. The realities were different in Uganda, though by this time, I was accustomed to loss and sudden moves. This time there was a missing piece in my puzzle. Why in the world Uganda? There are so many dialects in Uganda, that in one compound alone there might be three tribes using three different dialects. A few people spoke British English with a heavy accent from their dialects, which made it more difficult for us to pitch our momentary tent. We were on the street again—refugees in Kampala, Uganda!

Someone had told me that the best way to check if a wound is well healed, is to pinch it. Life squeezed my emotional wounds and found out that I was not healed yet. The very familiar feelings--feeling lost, angry, bitter, and fearful, climbed up from their hiding places and took over suddenly. I felt so disappointed with God and so confused. It felt as if I was back to the beginning again, only the setting was different. For a while, I struggled, trying to figure out what went wrong. What had I done to deserve this? I felt as if I was weaned prematurely. How could the good God let me go through another episode of this kind? I thought that it was over!

Logically, nothing made sense. Too many of us are at war within ourselves. When that happens, some questions arise, such as: Where do you go when you feel as though God has disappointed you? What do you do when you feel violated and wounded by God? People who are logical, like I used to be, have difficulty walking by faith or submitting to the will of God. If you relate to some of these feelings, I want you to know that you are not alone. So many people feel like that at one point or have been there somehow, that they don't say it because it sounds unspiritual to have these feelings. I committed to telling my story truthfully, so, stand with me and let the truth set you free. I searched my heart and studied the word of God to find something to hang on to; I learned that God's wisdom makes no "earthly" sense.

I remembered what the Lord spoke to me prior to fleeing to Uganda, which didn't make sense back then, but this time it made sense.

"I will bring the blind by the way they did not know; and I will lead them in the paths they have not known. I will make darkness light before them, and crooked places straight. These things I will do for them, and not forsake them." Isaiah 42:16

The knowledge of His love for me overwhelmed me and changed the way I was seeing my new life as a refugee in Kampala. Life wasn't going to be easy, but I was not alone. I knew without a shadow of a doubt that the Lord Himself was behind my fleeing to Uganda, and it made a huge difference in my attitude and the way I approached every day's challenges.

I was soon to learn total dependency on God and His mercy--how truly to trust in God's faithfulness and provision for every need. This was going to be hard because of some trusting issues I had from my previous life's experience.

Besides, anyone who knows me will tell you that I am stubborn with my "logic." I am a doer and have wasted time helping God to be God in my life. As funny as it sounds, I have been like a sheep showing the shepherd the way to go.

A few days after settling in Kampala, Uganda, my husband decided to go back to his country to sell everything left and bring the money to sustain us. I was afraid that he might not come back—that it might be just a way to abandon me and the girls. There was nothing I could do or say to keep him from going. He left us with a friend—a former colleague. This man had his own family (a wife, three children and a brother) to take care of. I was eight months pregnant with my fourth child and had three little girls. That how he left me.

Then the day came when I went into labor. The man of the house had traveled. His wife ignored me. (She had never had children. She was raising the kids from his first marriage.) I sent my oldest daughter to another Congolese family that lived in the same compound. The man, Emmanuel, and his wife, came over, and we sat there figuring out how to get me to the hospital. This man went to the landlord and asked for a ride. The landlord agreed to take me on one condition. We must go immediately because he could not drive in the night. I hugged my three girls and whispered to my oldest, who was then seven years old, to stay close to her sisters, lock the bedroom door when they go to sleep, and be nice to the lady of the house no matter what happens. My ride left me at the entrance to the hospital because if you took someone to the hospital, you might be held responsible for the bill and the care of the person. So, no one was going to be held responsible for me. I gathered my little English and made my way through a sea of people and went to the front to explain that I was in labor. They took me to the labor and delivery department. I reached there about six o' clock in the evening and was shown a bed to share with another woman. This was a section for low and poor people. It was a free place and the care we got was very limited. It was dirty and stunk horribly. I refused to sit on that bed. I put the bag of my baby's stuff on my back and stuck my ticket on the bed as a way to reserve my spot and then went outside. I never went back. I heard the Nursing students who took me there talking about me in the Ugandan language, saying, "Oh dear, this woman is very beautiful and clean. She shouldn't be in this section," and the other one responded saying that it is because I couldn't

144

pay. They spoke about me saying that I was a refugee from Rwanda and that was why I was beautiful and clean. When I made eye contact, they came over and introduced themselves as "Nakityo and Rosemary." They showed me the way to go when I was ready to deliver and told me they would be watching for me.

Through the night, I walked up and down the hallways of Nsambya Hospital. When the contractions would kick in, I would grab the stair rails and whisper, "Lord, help me!" A couple of times I sat down in exhaustion, but not for long, because the thought of leaving my other children behind was my motivation to keep going. I was committed to delivering the baby the same night and going back. It was around 1:00 A.M. and still my contractions were too far apart. I was discouraged and began to talk to the baby in my womb. "Baby, please come. We have to go back to your sisters; they're all alone."

Somehow, I wandered and kept going, praying, and crying. I went far beyond the labor and delivery zone, not knowing. I kept praying or maybe murmuring. The time went fast and something happened. The contractions became too frequent. Suddenly, I wanted to get inside of the room where I was shown, but couldn't find it. I panicked and started running. Then my water broke and I couldn't walk anymore. I took hold of a pillar and screamed. A man who was passing by carrying boxes in a wheel barrow, saw me. He came running and he quickly emptied the wheel barrow and put me in the cart rushing to get me to the place. He spoke the local language, but I don't know what he said.

Inside, we met Nakityo. She laughed when the man told where he found me. I was rushed to the bed and before I could lie down I dropped on my knees and had my baby girl. The last contractions were not painful because I was screaming, begging for a sheet or something to kneel on. The baby was born on the dirty floor. I was concerned that I didn't feel the pain of her birth. It was 5:30 in the morning when I was taken to another dirty bed, but this time I had no choice. I was exhausted and Nakityo took the bag off my back and took care of the baby. She then wrapped both of us in a hospital gown. I tried to stay awake, not wanting my baby to lie on the dirty bed, but she was all tied up on my chest by the so-called sterile gown.

Abigail was born! She was very little and frail. She is the last of four beautiful daughters with which God has entrusted me. Since it was the weekend, I was kept there even though I wanted to leave and go take care of my other children whom I had left alone at the mercy of neighbors. Early Monday morning, while getting ready to leave, I saw Arlette, my oldest daughter, running to me, followed by the neighbor—the man who dropped me off that Friday. He told me that my daughter wanted to know where they took me, that she cried all the time thinking that they had killed me, and that she wanted to see where they took me. He immediately left the room leaving us there.

We waited there and a few hours later, the hospital Nurse came by with the discharge papers, including the birth certificate of my youngest daughter. I noticed that they wrote her date of birth on the day that I was admitted, instead of the real time of birth. I got to the hospital on Friday, December 03, at 7:00 P.M. and she was born early Saturday on December 04. When I asked the Nurse in charge to change it, I was dismissed because I was a social outcast who had no case. The hospital was not going to get paid for the service given to me. I was an illegal case in Uganda. I had eaten nothing since Friday and had only had a little water given by the student Nurses when they were passing out medications. No one knew how I got there and no one cared enough to ask if I had help or food to eat.

I gathered my strength and held the baby in my

arms. Arlette followed me as we left the hospital. Outside the hospital gate, we were welcomed by the morning heat and so much noise, we got on the bus and went home.

The neighborhood's kids and my own children were waiting for us. They were happy, dancing and singing, and wanting to know if it's a boy or a girl. I was home at last!

The days that followed my coming back from the hospital were unpleasant. The host couple was challenged in their relationship. There was tension between the man and his wife. It was known to everyone that they had always been unhappy. I didn't want to be in the middle of that unhealthy atmosphere. I kept my little girls in our room. They played there and I prayed, pleading for the Lord to show me the way out.

One evening, I took a walk outside the compound with all my daughters, just to get out of the room. We strolled the neighborhood almost every evening and that evening was no different. Holding back tears, I prayed silently, "Lord, help me know where to go and what to do." It seemed as if I had made an emotional U-turn; it was a deja vue feeling of perplexity, worry, and the kind of helplessness I once experienced when I got to Zaire years ago.

On the way back from that evening

promenade, we met the Landlord's wife. She was a very nice woman with kindness you only find in people who really know God. She was happy to see me and the girls. She looked at the newborn and apologized for not having been able to come see the baby. She asked me if we still wanted to move out since we were now getting bigger (four children…) I told her that my husband had left and gone back to Congo, but if I could move, I would do it immediately. She told me that they had a two bedroom apartment that would soon be ready. I asked how soon? She told me that they still needed to install water and electricity, otherwise it's not ready. We walked back together and visited the "not ready" apartment. It was in the middle of a banana plantation, a little bit farther from the Landlord's house, but closer to the goat's manger, as it had been designed for a caretaker.

A few days later, I sent a note with my oldest daughter asking the Landlord's wife if they would allow me to move into that apartment in spite of the lack of water and electricity. I met her and her husband. I explained that I would like to assume responsibility instead of being a burden to the family that hosted us. The Landlord was ex-military and a very noble man. He told me that since the apartment was not ready for lease due to the lack of water and electricity, I should stay in it for free. I would fetch water in their compound and use paraffin or candles for light, hoping that when my husband came back, we would be able to afford a better place to live. I packed my few things and took my children and we moved into the unfinished place.

I took this as an answer from God. It was better for me to separate nicely with that family than to wait to be thrown outside. This way we kept contact and our relationship got even better. They visited and brought us food once in a while, and I organized prayer meetings in my place and started a prayer cell right around our candlelight "electricity".

It was a two-bedroom studio; the two bedrooms were separated by the empty living room with dirty concrete for a floor. The kitchen and bathroom were outside. There was no utility service. It was just incomplete and not ready to live in. I scrubbed the floor and disinfected the bathroom. I hung on each wall the pine branches to bring in a fresh smell and to kill the small flying insects and mosquitos. I moved in with my little girls, two suitcases, and two mattresses. That same day, I managed to buy a saucepan, two plates, and a washbasin; a new life had begun—another step of faith.

"Faith is taking the first step even when you don't see the whole staircase." Martin Luther King, Jr.

Real faith is madness! This was suicidal! Four little kids on the road to nowhere. There have been a few times in my life when I tested the word of God. This was one of them. I knew that if the Lord didn't come through for me, I was going to watch my children die, one by one.

Not having much to do, those days were spent in prayer and searching the scriptures. I will forever be thankful toward the Lord for coming thru on time, because I was committed to doing anything to keep my children alive. It is one thing to know about God and talk about Him; it is another thing to know God and talk of His goodness. The word many use is "grace." I am a woman who has been graced by God! As days went by, I began having a thought, "There must be help out there, but how to get that help: where to go?"

In Kampala \ UGANDA,1998

Chapter Ten—Following the Shepherd

One night, I couldn't sleep. I was tossing and turning, and couldn't take my mind off the urge I had been feeling for days. I knew I should try to go to the city to check on the status of my refugee's case, but I had no means to get there. It caused so much pain that I could feel my chest tightening and cramps in my stomach. It was unbearable; it kept me wide-awake. My little girls were asleep beside me in the small dark room we shared. Their small snoring made me realize that I was not alone. I stretched my arm on my left side to feel three of them peacefully asleep, and the baby was on my right side sleeping on a separate small bed made of a folded blanket. They were all there alive, but for how long? This thought brought a knot to my throat. "I can't cry," I told myself. For a long time, I held the tears, afraid that if I allowed myself to cry, the stream in my head wouldn't stop. I slowly rolled off the pitiful bed I shared with my daughters, making sure not to wake them up. As I walked out of the room, the squeaky door gave me away and my oldest daughter, who was then about eight years old, asked me, "Mama, are you going to pee?"

"Yes, Baby," I responded.

"Do you want me to watch for you?" she asked. I told her that I was fine.

"Go back to sleep, Baby," I said, fighting to keep my voice reassuring.

Outside, I sat there in the peaceful night. Oh, how I wished my heart to be as quiet as that summer night! The moon was high and clear and the wind was cool and so gentle. Looking up in the sky, I knew that the night was spent. It was maybe about three in the morning. The new day was ahead. I could hear the crickets and frogs singing their songs afar and near me everything was still except my heartbeat.

My eyes fixed on the beautiful moon. I couldn't help but admire the mystery of the creation, and there were neither pillars nor strings to hold the moon up in sky. There must be a God who is the maker of all. "Help me, God," I whispered. I just sat there for what seemed like an eternity.

A scripture came to my mind. "I will bring the blind by the way they didn't know. I lead them in paths they have not known. I will make darkness light before them And crooked places straight, these things I will do for them, And I will not forsake them." Back then, I didn't know where the scripture was from. I just knew it was in the Bible. It was brought to my heart as if a recorder played it to me.

The urge to go to UNHCR (United Nations High Commission on Refugees) was so powerful I had to make a decision that morning. I was to go there. I didn't have transport money and didn't want to leave my little girls alone. Then, like the two lepers in the Bible (II Kings 7), I told myself, "If I stay here, I will see my children dying one by one, and if I go and get no help, I will come back with a clear conscience." With the last remaining borrowed money, I took the bus that morning and headed to Kampala.

The money was not enough for the bus to get me right at the gate of the UNHCR office. I had to walk the remaining few miles on foot. I walked as fast as I could, trying to find my way around a sea of people, cars, buses, and motorcycles (Bodabodas). A thought flew into my mind that if I couldn't make it back to my house, I would have left four little girls all alone in the middle of nowhere. Fear grabbed me. Cold sweat and hot tears blinded my eyes and I had to use my T-shirt to wipe my face. I heard myself whispering, "Oh God, help me. Jesus help me." I kept on as fast as possible. Soon, I could see the big gate with the UNHCR inscription in blue, bold, and big letters. I had arrived!

When I made it to the gate, I was drenched with sweat. Due to the passage of the equator through the south central part of Kampala, the temperature is high all the year around. The heat is severe and due to Lake Victoria and the fishing activities that go on there, the humidity is also high, which makes it hard to breathe. I reached the gate sweating and almost out of breath. I approached the guard in uniform and gave him my name for the registry. With a gesture of his hand, he pointed the way. A long line of awaiting refugees was stretched out to a couple of feet from the gate; I made my way to the end of the line with so much discouragement and stood there as long as my legs could hold on.

Around us, all kind of business went on as always. Some were selling tobacco cigarettes, some were selling bananas and peanuts, some were selling cakes and water in Ziploc bags, and all these were covered with dust and flies. A few names were called and taken into the compound. I had no hope of being called because time was advancing and I was among the last in that long line.

I quit the line to go find a place to sit in the shade. As I sat down, I felt cramps in my legs. My feet were swollen and the sandals I wore were cutting into my skin. As I looked at my missing toenails, I was reminded of how rough my journey had been since the day I left my home country in the Spring of 1994, and four years later I was still on the run searching for refuge. I whispered, "Lord, how long?"

My self-pity moment was interrupted. The gate sprang open and a gentleman rushed out in anger—screaming and cursing. I realized that he spoke French. I ran after him asking what was happening inside there. I came to know that he was from Zaire (Congo), and he had given some bribe to a certain woman who supposedly worked there to have his name added on the interviews list. When he came to see her, she was not willing to receive him, and he made a scene and was escorted out by security. On the way out, someone gave him a business card of someone who could possibly help him, which meant another bribe to give. He was very outraged.

I took time to look at him as he murmured in anger. He was very clean and well dressed. He didn't smell and had no dust on his shoes. He must be one ambitious man who just wants a way out of Africa to any western country to fulfill his ambitions, I thought. I told him that my husband was from Zaire, too. For a few minutes we spoke of how Uganda was more corrupted than Congo. As he spoke, he kept waiving the business card with a disgraced facial expression. He was about to shred it when I asked him to let me have it. As he handed it to me, his motorcycle ride arrived and he left me there with a piece of paper that changed my entire journey.

It was about a quarter to 4:00 P.M. when I made my way back to the security guard at the entrance of the gate. I asked him to tell me how to get to the address that was on the business card. He told me that it was a few blocks down from the UNHCR office. I took off running as fast as possible. I reached the place a few minutes before the closing time, which was 5:00 P.M. Out of breath, I entered without knocking to find myself in a very confined, small apartment. There were five people there, but due to the size of the room, it seemed as if a hundred pairs of eyes were looking at me. I stood there sweating, perplexed, for what seemed like an eternity. Then, one young white man stood up and came to me asking what I needed. I showed him the card in my hand. He looked at an old, white woman with short, gray hair and eyeglasses and said, "Dr. Harrell Bond is in a meeting as you can see." I heard what he said, but I couldn't reply because I didn't know much English. I looked past the young man and made eye contact with an expressionless woman and in exhaustion I simply said, "Please, please."

She didn't move nor change her expression. She said, "From Ethiopia? Somalia? What language do you speak?"

"French," I replied. She stood up and came to me. She looked tall when she was in the chair. I noticed that she was shorter than I was and very skinny with tough skin. She walked past me and on the kitchen counter she took a piece of paper and wrote, "Come here on Tuesday at 10:00 A.M." She gave the paper to me and took the card I had. It was dirty from sweaty hands that had carried it all day. She looked at it with a smile and she looked at me and simply shook her head. She folded both together and handed them back to me. I stood there before her not knowing what to say because of the language limitations. She looked in my eyes intensely and said, "Understand?"

With tears rolling down my cheeks I said, "Thank you, thank you," but I didn't move. I didn't know how to tell her that I had no means to come back there on Tuesday. In fact, I didn't know how to go back to my place that day. She opened the kitchen drawer and took a cigarette and immediately her expression changed to what seemed like a smile. She took some money from the drawer and handed it to me saying, "For the bus to come back on Tuesday."

More tears streamed from my eyes as I witnessed a miracle unfolding before me. She showed me the time on her watch. I assume that she was reminding me to hurry up and go. She tapped on my shoulder in a reassuring gesture as she closed the door behind me. The money she gave me was the equivalent of $15 today. It was enough to get me home, get me some bread and eggs for the girls, and bring me back on Tuesday.

That night, after putting the girls to bed, I took a shower and sat down outside the door in the same place I had sat the night before. Trying to make sense out of the events that occurred during the day, I found myself wondering if it was a dream. Maybe I drifted in my mind; maybe nothing really happened. The blisters on my feet were a proof that it was real. Without electricity, I enjoyed the clarity of the moon. The sky was clear; the night was cool. I sat there meditating on what God did that day. It was a very intimate moment.

Over the weekend, I kept thinking about what happened and my mind would play games as usual, wondering if I was dreaming and when I woke up it would have been just a dream. On Monday night, I got ready for the following day. I made a meal for the girls, laid out their breakfast, lunch, and water. I explained to the oldest how things would go and prayed for the night, asking the Lord to be with us and thanking Him for what lay ahead for us.

On Tuesday, I was at the office an hour before the opening time. I found a spot in the shade by the Kiosk facing the entrance to the office, watching people going in and out. Then the time came and it was my turn! I knocked at the door and it opened! I stepped in and stood firmly there waiting to be acknowledged.

A few minutes later, the room was empty. I was sitting across the coffee table where the three were sitting. Then, Dr. Harrell Bond spoke to them in English and the young woman turned to me and spoke in a perfect French, which brought a smile to my face. She introduced herself. She was a lawyer soon-to-be from Oxford University. She had studied in France and came to Uganda recently to help the office to select cases that needed their intervention. Dr. Harrell Bond had asked her to work with me because I spoke French. The young man was also a law student in the Netherlands. We sat there for about three hours. I told my story in French while the young woman translated it into English. At the end of my story, Dr. Harrell Bond asked me to provide the names of the expatriates who were in charge of the nonprofit organizations I worked for before fleeing to Uganda, and their countries of origin, so I named a few. When I left that day, something was changed in me; "hope" was born. That hope carried me through the remaining time I stayed as a refuge in Kampala, Uganda. I gave them my Landlord's telephone number and was given some shillings, the equivalent of $30.00, for transport to the next meeting.

Two weeks later, I was back in the same office. I was welcomed by the smell of fresh coffee with cigarette smoke. The table was covered with papers and magazines. I sat down with the young woman. She told me that there was some good news. Before she could tell me, Dr. Harrell Bond came in with a big smile. She looked younger than the last time I saw her. I guess this was the work of Hope. Hope changes the way one sees things or situations. I was seeing through a new set of lenses; things were brightening up. I, myself, felt younger and smarter as I spoke to the group of lawyers. I felt as if I were a different person. She told me that one of the contacts I gave had responded and was willing to help in any way possible. She told me that someone accepted supporting me financially, and that she had some money to give to me. Thereafter, each month I would receive a certain amount to take care of my needs.

"I will bring the blind by a way they did not know; I will lead them in paths they have not known. I will make darkness light before them, And crooked places straight. These things I will do for them, And not forsake them." Isaiah 42:16

This scripture rang in my head so loudly that I thought it was audible to everyone around me. We reviewed the final version of my story. I signed it and sat there listening to their strategy about whom to call and how to go about this and that. For a while they spoke as if I were not there. With little to almost no English to understand fully what was being said, it was like I was in a vision, or a very good dream that I didn't want to wake up from.

That day, I walked away with an envelope of $110.00 in shillings and a promise to wait for a phone call from Dr. Harrell Bond. There have been few occasions like this in my life—a moment when I know I have no power over any decision concerning the next step in my life. One would think it to be a break, or a time for rest, but for someone like me, it is a restless moment— especially when one has had rough experiences in the past. Every day, I would check with my landlord to see if anyone had called for me and I begged him to not ignore any call because the call I was expecting was very important.

The day came and I got a message that said to be at the UNHCR office the next day at 10:00 A.M., having with me all my identification cards and those of anyone who was my dependent. I was given the name of a person to meet with and told to ask for that individual right when I got to the gate.

The same gate behind which so many people had spent months, and I myself had stood for long hours waiting for nothing, that day opened and I was escorted through it like a VIP.

In the long lobby, I met with a UNHCR worker whose origin I assume was Indian. He greeted me with a big handshake and a welcoming smile. In his office, he read me the report that was sent to him from the "Uganda Refugees Project" and asked me to provide him my identity and those of

164

my entire household. Multiple copies were made and in few minutes I signed the agreement to abide under the UNHCR protection as long as I remained in Uganda. I would receive a minimum of financial aid for food, since I was not in a refugee camp, and my children were to attend a local school close to where I lived. Sitting on the bus going back home that day, my prayer was, "Please, Lord, don't wake me up."

It was like a dream! To the day I left Uganda, I lacked nothing! The Lord faithfully provided for me and protected me.

This part of our journey I called "Following the Shepherd". In Uganda we began to live the twenty-third psalm in an amazing way. We were scared as you can imagine—Uganda is different from all the places we had been, and our needs were much more extensive with four vulnerable kids, but each day there was a whisper in my heart, "Trust in the Lord. He will not let you down."

Chapter Eleven--Psalm 23
The Lord is my Shepherd

When you have faced the worst there is in life and come to embrace the love of God, the way you approach life is totally different. There was peace and hope in my heart though it was hard to explain to my husband. I suffered to see him depressed over something God Himself initiated. I could not find a convincing way to tell him that we would be all right. He sometimes reminds me of Thomas, the Disciple (doubting Thomas). If he can't see it, it is not there, and it is not there until it is there—not when they said it will be there. The events of God's faithfulness began to unfold in our lives in a magical way. The money from the humanitarian in the U. K. who knew us in the Congo kept flowing month after month until we left Uganda to come to America.

We read the book of Exodus and we think it is a true story; it happened, but it was a one-time done deal. However, it is about the everlasting God who provides for His people;

"Forty years you sustained them in the wilderness, they lacked nothing; their clothes did not wear out, and their feet did not swell." Nehemiah 9:21

It may sound like a fairy tale to you because it did sound like a good one to my daughters when I shared with them how the Lord showed us His faithfulness, but it is as true as the air I breathe; "their clothes did not wear out and their feet did not swell!" Right! The clothes stretched and adjusted with the growth of their bodies; the shoes on their feet grew with them. It is amazing what God can do.

For two and a half years, faithfully God provided for all our needs; we lacked nothing. We were able to afford a fair place to live (a two bedroom apartment with a huge living room, electricity and running water). Three of our daughters were in school. We were able to feed them two good meals a day. All these were the benefits of having the Lord as a good shepherd.

Psalm 34:10 tells us also that, "*Young lions lack and suffer of hunger but those who seek the Lord shall not lack of anything good.*" I heard someone saying that when it is God's will, the bill is His. You will never understand this until you get down on your knees and give your hands up in surrender. "If it is your will, it is also your bill."

My daughters, Kampala\UGANDA, 2000

He Makes Me Lie Down in Green Pastures

David was a Shepherd; therefore he knew how to relate to a good Shepherd—GOD! He knew the responsibilities upon the Shepherd's shoulder—the love and care of a true Shepherd. He knew that he could trust in the love, protection, and care of God. His peace and quietness were found in the midst of a pasture that was one of a kind. I grew up in the land of a "thousand hills" (Rwanda). The agriculture and pasturing are two basic livelihoods. I know maybe a little about the pasture; green or not green; there is no quietness in the pasture full of a flock. I believe that the life of David was saturated by the presence of God, the full dependency upon Him and the full trust in the care and protection of the Lord. When the Lord satisfies you, you can find peace in the midst of a battlefield.

You may find yourself in the factory or in the market. Believe me, when the presence of God has saturated your life, you can experience a fellowship with Him with undivided attention and that will be your "green pasture" (a place of fellowship, meditation etc...).

I lay down under the hot sun of the sub-Sahara desert in Uganda. It was my green pasture. I was fed on the goodness of the Lord. In the midst of nowhere, I found the peace that surpasses all understanding; the peace of knowing that I have a shepherd. I am not alone; He has promised to care for me and to lead me. Like a sheep, I just followed.

I may not be able to explain all the facts concerning my journey, but what I determined to do is to lay it down for you, so you can journey with me through this book. Again, each one of us is on a journey. We are in different places and our experiences are unique, but wherever you are in your journey, I can assure you that everything I have written is true. Three of my girls were sent to school. My last baby was few months old. I was advised to stay home for my security's sake, so I spent a great deal of time reading and meditating on the word of God when my husband was in the city following the case at the UNHCR and my kids were at school. I found and enjoyed the benefit of lying down in the green pasture. To me, there has been something very healing about the silence, the quietness, the stillness of my soul, bringing all of my being into the presence of the Lord. In the green pastures, David found peace and was inspired to write these beautiful psalms.

He spoke of restoration and healing; he poured out his heart to the Lord.

In my green pasture, I came to know the Shepherd. I learned to trust in His care and guidance and He began the work of healing and restoration in my life.

No one can predict what you will live through when you accept that you will lie down in whatever pasture He makes for you. The sure thing is that there is a place for you—a place of meeting the shepherd—a place where you will come to realize that you cannot keep going until you will reach a dead end. In that place you will pitch a tent and with knees down and hands up you will say, "I am done, Lord, take over the wheel of my life." It feels good to submit to the Shepherd's will because he pays the bills. The Lord is my Shepherd, I shall not want!

He Guides Me in Paths of Righteousness

It is interesting to watch the shepherding of sheep, because they are not "smart." The shepherd goes before them and they follow, otherwise, they will just stand still and make noises. On the other side, when shepherding cows, the Shepherd goes behind the herd. They follow the trail (they know the routine).

The whole time we lived in Uganda, I was overwhelmed by the ways God cared for us. Every day had a picture of itself with true the goodness of God renewed each morning. I had much to learn about God's character. I read and meditated on the word of God. I learned to listen to the Shepherd. *"I know My sheep and am known by My own... my sheep hear My voice, and I know them, and they follow Me."* (John 10: 14, 27)

I immersed myself in the Bible. It was during this time that I formed a firm foundation for my life built on the character of God and not on anything else. I felt whole. God was leading me to a new path; His path.

God makes a path. He provides guidance and feeds us in the wilderness, that we may confess His glorious name as long as we breathe.

Many times I have had no guide, no house; I was homeless. I had no food, no coat for my back on rainy days, no friends. In Him, I found it all.

It became clear that there were so many suffering people in the neighborhood where we lived. Some were refugees like us. Kampala is a metropolitan capital for refugees from Sudan, Somalia, Ethiopia, Kenya, Rwanda, Congo, Burundi, etc. There were so many who were lost and hopeless. I felt led to attend to them in my spare time. Out of the fullness of my heart, I felt so rich, and wanted to share with the whole world what I was learning. "God is good and He is in the business of restoring lives!"

Soon my living room was transformed into a church. We met on a regular basis. We offered our home as a place of rest for so many. We shared with them what we had--especially the word of God. So many people gave their lives to Christ in my very living room. Among them was my own husband. We prayed for each one of us and trusted the Lord to meet our daily needs.

We became a bridge for many who were in transit to different destinations. Some were sent to Canada, Australia, the Netherlands, the UK and the USA. At one point I grew concerned. I saw people coming and going. Their prayer requests were granted. I told them about the God whose faithfulness never fails. They were going while we were left there. The peace of God wrapped me in an amazing way! I felt as though even if I never left Uganda, through me, the Lord was doing something great. It had a tremendous impact on people. So many people were finding hope. They learned to run to God for all their needs. It is what I taught; you can only give what you have got; you can only lead to where you have been led. So I did. I taught the love and power of God, restoration and healing of broken hearts, and I spoke of surrendering to the will of God. Well, it worked!

Like a shepherd, God supplies our needs (Psalms 23:1). Some of us know for certain that God is our provider. Our trials have been so difficult that if it had not been for heaven's action, you and I would never have been delivered. We have sunk so deep in poverty that many of our friends have stayed away. If you are like me, you know there is only one arm that is able to lift you up. Perhaps you have been reduced to such conditions that all you can do is pray. You wrestle at the throne and seek for answers, but nothing is coming. If you have used every effort to free yourself but darkness covers your way again and again and your hope is vanishing, remember, the Lord is a good Shepherd.

When I was in Bukavu, Congo, I spoke about the love of God from head knowledge, but this time I drew from the fullness of my heart, a heart full of gratitude. I was a new person. "The Lord He is my Shepherd, I shall not want." I spoke from my experiences and relationship with the Lord. I knew the Shepherd. I was being fed by Him. It is one thing to know *about* God and another thing to *know* God. He is your Shepherd when you rest and feed in His pasture. This way you can bear witness of His goodness, faithfulness, and love. Let Him lead. You will never get lost.

I Will Fear No Evil, For You are With Me

When we arrived in Kampala, we were welcomed by malaria. Because of many parasites, the heat and moisture; all of our four girls were admitted to the hospital at once. Financially, we were not in a position to get good treatment for our children. We visited different small clinics in the neighborhood where we lived but no improvement was seen. We didn't know where to turn but to the Lord. We had no money to take them for better treatment. We cried every night when we were alone—Leon and I. We poured out our hearts to God. We had lost material things; we couldn't afford to lose our children, but since we did not have the money needed for their treatment, Lord, we believe that you can miraculously heal them. If it is your will to take them, help us to accept it. We had just lost all the money we had on the fake visa where we were scammed, and then malaria came while we were trying to find our way in Kampala. I saw pain and failure in Leon's eyes; I have not seen him in this state since the night we were fleeing from Rwanda to Congo.

It was one Saturday as I went outside to cry out to God early in the morning when I took the Bible with me. As I cried I opened it randomly and read the last line of the sentence where Jesus told Mary and Martha at the tomb of their brother Lazarus, *"If you believe, you will see the glory of God,"* (John 11:40). I came back to the house and told Leon the same thing. He thought that I had lost my mind. Naturally, there was no way to expect anything good to come out of that situation. We were in the midst of nowhere. Nobody knew us in that place; we had no money; we were helpless. I sensed the word of God coming alive in my soul that morning as never before, when I read those words of the Lord Jesus to Mary and Martha. They came alive and vibrated in my heart. I wish I could tell you that I heard them with my ears, which would make sense, but the truth is my heart captured the message while my mind was still confused. I wanted so much to believe, but it didn't come easily. I went outside again to hide and cry. Then, I met the landlord's wife. She asked me how we had been doing because she hadn't seen the smart girls for a while. "Are they away?" she asked. I told her that they had been so sick with malaria, that they were not doing well at all. Tears flew from my eyes as I said these words. She asked if she could come to visit. She followed me to my small studio behind their big mansion.

When she saw the girls, she spoke in her language and rushed out without a word. She came back with her husband and told us to get ready for we must go to the big hospital in the city immediately. We tried to tell them that we had no money, but they were already hauling us in the car. They drove us across the town to the best private clinic in the town. For coming in with this business man, we were given a large private room. They set up four beds and a couch; all the girls were admitted right away. We saw doctors and nurses running back and forth transporting our children one after another for transfusions of blood and water. Leon and I were scared because we didn't know how we would tell them that we couldn't pay for every service provided. They spoke their local language between themselves and a few words of English to us. They knew that we didn't know much of English. They kept saying that our third daughter was not making it. They were losing her. In few minutes, they told us that they couldn't save her. She was dying.

I screamed in my language. I prayed that God would send an angel to revive my little girl. I was running like a mad woman in that hospital. I rushed into the urgent care where my third daughter was being treated and found the nurse disconnecting the IV's. She tried to hold me down to no avail. I jumped from the floor to the roof. Then, from nowhere, an old man appeared. I didn't hear him approaching as I was screaming. I just smelled his funny sweat. He began praying in the local language and in other tongues. The amazing thing is that I was able to understand every word he was saying. I don't know how it happened but it is true. He was praying and binding the spirit of death in the room. After what seemed an eternity, as I laid over the body of my little girl, I felt something moving under the covers. She was looking at me awake and alive. I screamed and the nurses came back in. We were all astounded.

I looked to see the old guy who prayed with me. He was nowhere to be seen. No one had seen him except my husband and I. You may not believe that angels exist. It's o.k. I am not going to change your belief. I am sharing with you mine. The angels of the Lord are active in service to those who call for help. In my weakness and ignorance, the Lord sent an angel to sustain us and to break the arrow of death that the enemy had pointed to destroy and kill my children.

Again, you do not have to believe my story; you can even tear out this page from the book if you find it odd. I will not be offended.

We were in the hospital for five days. The landlord and his wife took care of us. They brought us food and a few things we needed. We walked out of that hospital five days later debt free, with all our children well healed. Malaria never came back to our home for the entire time we stayed in Uganda. Today, I can say with confidence, *"Yea, though I walk through the valley of the shadow of death, I will fear no evil for you are with me."* (Psalm 23:4)

Because I walked with the Shepherd through the valley of the shadow of death and came out with no harm, I came to know that His rod and His staff are not designed to beat me up. They are not to punish me but are designed to reassure me of His protection. It is painful enough to find ourselves going through the valley of the shadow of death. Tell me why the good Shepherd would comfort his sheep by beating them up? He will keep them above the fear, agony, and the sense of being lost in the valley. In my native language the word "comfort" comes with a more reassuring sense or meaning (guhumuriza). It is reassuring to know that my Shepherd is well equipped and has what is needed to protect me while escorting me through the valley._The "comfort" of knowing that the Lord is there is contentment! The word "comfort" in Hebrew means "Nacham": to console, to have deep empathy. It also means "Paraklesis," which translates as a strengthening presence. This is enough to assure that the rod and staff in the hand of the shepherd are designed to protect and not to hurt.

How much I wanted to shout, "I told you if you believe, you will see the glory of God!"

During our stay in Uganda, the Lord revealed Himself to us in many ways. Like the psalmist, *"Many, O Lord my God, are your wonderful works which you have done; and your thoughts toward us cannot be recounted to you in order. If I would declare and speak of them, they are more than can be numbered."* (Psalm 40:5).

Today, as I look back to this part of my journey, I am happy to say that am glad I have a Shepherd and I chose to follow Him. I do not know how we could have made it otherwise.

I have received deliverance in many marvelous ways from so unseen a hand, from so unlikely a source, and under strange circumstances. Yet, the deliverances were so perfect, so complete, and so wonderful. I wish I had the words to explain the full measure of this experience. I can say now with full confidence that, "The Lord is my Shepherd; I shall fear no evil."

Being comforted by the rod and the staff of the Shepherd had a confusing sense in my life before experiencing it. I have always thought of both as weapons to be used to discipline me when I do wrong. I came, however, to know that the Shepherd uses these to protect and to secure his flock from devouring powers. Moses led with a rod but not to use it to discipline God's people. He used it to break up the waters of the Red Sea. We see the Lord sending His staff to protect and keep company with His people while being tortured and afflicted in the story of Daniel and the story of the three Hebrew boys. If you can see it, the Good Shepherd is always prepared to fight for our lives.

You Prepare a Table Before Me in the Presence of My Enemies

Writing this book has not been easy at all. Each sentence reminds me of a lifetime struggle. It is as if I was pinching at my almost-healed scars. It becomes too hard to believe that there is some pain in remembering some of the more unpleasant episodes, but moreover, there is a sense of, "Wow! I made it out of it!"

Let me take you to our last days in Uganda. The Shepherd leads the sheep where He pleases, and certainly, He will lead them according to His will. When the time came that we were called to go to the British Embassy for health checkups and immunizations, we also had a brief American culture orientation. Nobody was supposed to know about our departure for security reasons, but people who were in the same orientation or those who had seen us at the Embassy knew something. Then it was out!

Going to America was like going to heaven! This caused jealousy among our prayer group and neighbors. People stopped speaking to us. They were angry and hateful and they accused us of being hypocrites because we couldn't tell them about our big move to America. No matter how much we explained it, it didn't ease their hate. It was just a useless defense to their jealousy.

We received all kind of threats. Someone told us to be careful because people were plotting to kidnap our children just a day before the travel. Our landlord threatened us to throw us out because he had just found a longtime tenant and we were no longer any good to him. The chief of the community paid us a visit saying that we had dwelt in the place for more than we should without paying the tax to the local office. We were refugees. There was no such law as this! It was one thing after another. We stayed on our knees thanking the Lord for the work He was doing, but with fear on every side. We didn't know what people could do one day or another.

Two days before we were scheduled to travel, two of our daughters got sick. They had measles. They were running a high fever and their entire bodies were covered by those measles. It is impossible to travel with those conditions, especially for the safety of the public. We almost lost hope!

We had to leave the house for the new tenant, we had no money for a hotel room while waiting for the measles to clear up, and surely we were not going to board the plane in that condition. We were in the experience of the Red Sea!

"Do not be afraid, stand still, and see the salvation of the Lord, which He will accomplish for you today. For the Egyptians whom you see today, you shall see again no more forever. The Lord will fight for you, and you shall hold your peace." (Exodus 14:13-14)

The day of our departure when the girls woke up, the measles were gone! They didn't have any fever. It was as if nothing had ever happened. They were healed!

After being in place for two years, surely there were people who became very attached to us more than others. There were those who were consistent in the weekly prayer meeting and those who got involved in our lives in one way or another, such as hair dressers, shoe repairmen, and Bodaboda drivers (motorbike). We decided to invite them for a goodbye time.

After packing the few things we needed for the journey, we separated the remaining stuff, designating it to each of our friends. Everything we had we gave away. After all, no one comes to America with a bed and a bucket. We thanked them for being good neighbors and friends and we asked them to forgive us where we had offended them. Then we called each one to give them these gifts. It was an emotional moment! Some were sad and crying, some were jumping for joy for the gifts they received, but all were touched. To the ones who had children, we gave all our children's stuff (shoes, clothes, toys); to the others we gave beds and mattresses; to others we gave the kitchen stuff. An old lady came to me and said, "A woman never gives away all her saucepans. You must keep the oldest one." I smiled and told her that where I was going there were many beautiful saucepans. Later, I was told that in their culture, she meant to tell me that wherever I go I will always be a woman—a housekeeper, a homemaker and a caregiver.

The day of the departure, they all came and brought the entire community to send us off. We prayed for the trip and we asked a blessing for them for the kindness they had shown to us. They also blessed us and sent us off. Many were crying. Some others volunteered to escort us to the airport.

Once again we saw the work and peace of God; we knew then that a chapter of our lives was over, but a new one was yet to begin.

It is not unusual to face hardship in the same manner we did. Our last days in Uganda reminded me of the children of Israel when they were about to cross over to the Promised Land. Pharaoh and his army would not let them go. They had an experience of what I call "facing the Red Sea." In the Rwandan language it means that the enemy might not kill you, but he may delay your journey, however, when the good Shepherd is at work, all things work together for our benefit. We crossed over our Red Sea.

We arrived in the USA safe and sound. We landed at the Nashville airport on September 25, 2000, and since then we have made Tennessee our home. I will never be thankful enough to the Lord and the Americans for giving me a place to call home again. For about six years, I moved from one place to another, from one country to another, seeking a safe place to raise my children—a place where no one will point me out and call me a cockroach, where my children would not be spoken of in such manner as this: "Little snakes are venomous as well as the big snakes."

For many years I wondered why we wound up in America, not in Canada or France, where we could speak French, since French is our language. I was led to the land of freedom. I accepted and followed the Shepherd.

The 23rd Psalm ends beautifully.

Surely Goodness and Mercy Shall Follow Me

Mercy in Hebrew is "chesed," which is the unfailing, steadfast, covenant love of God. It is similar to "Grace" in the New Testament in some way. The key to God's provision is His presence. The goodness of God is based on God's character. He is GOOD! When He is present in one's life, there is no lack. The whole time we were traveling, I had people to carry my stuff; people volunteered to help me with my children—even the hostess on the flight fell in love with my girls. The favor of God was at work in our lives. His mercy and goodness was following us and chasing us. It was noticeable! One could think that I knew all these individuals.

Our God is a covenant keeper. When He said, "I will not leave you nor forsake you," He meant it. We must believe in His unchanging character.

And I Will Dwell in the House of the Lord Forever

I must admit that I dislike the way this Psalm has been misinterpreted, especially when it is used in funeral services. I may be wrong, but to my understanding, the beauty of this refreshing pastoral psalm reflects absolute trust and peaceful confidence in God. It is divided into two descriptions; the Shepherd (vs. 1-4) and the Host (vs. 5-6).

The picture of God as Shepherd is fulfilled and completed in the person of Jesus Christ, who is presented as the redeeming Good Shepherd, (John 10:1), the resurrected Great Shepherd (Heb. 13:20), and the returning Chief Shepherd (1 Pet.5:4). In the house of the Lord there is peace—Shalom (rest, harmony, wholeness). I have got it! This does not mean that I have made it to heaven. Things happen. Storms and thunders roar, but deep in my heart, I know this also shall pass. I came to understand that the "peace"—Shalom—is a gift of and from the Lord Himself.

Chapter Twelve—Welcome to America and the American Dream

We arrived at the Nashville airport on September 25th, 2000, at 10:00 P.M. No one was there to welcome us! I was exhausted emotionally and physically and my children were exhausted as well. I carried on me an IOM (International Organization for Migration) package in which were my Immigration files. Separately, I had been given a phone number for the organization that sponsored my family. There was a staff member from another agency receiving refugees settled by that other agency. He told us that we were not theirs. We panicked! We gave him the number and asked him to make a call for us.

A few minutes later we were on board riding with Langley Grandberry and Miss Wanda Faye (may the Lord give her soul everlasting peace). Both were from World Relief. We were sent to a large Presbyterian church in Nashville Tennessee. We lived in a guesthouse by the church. We were frustrated and confused!

Our days were filled with so many good things: an excursion to the zoo, visiting with new friends from that church. So many people were signing up to take us places, from day one our days were filled up with different activities. All this was good—maybe too good to be true, but they were unnecessary, especially when planned without our participation in the planning. Few took time to ask what we needed or what we would like to do. Others filled us in their agenda. With those many years on the run, in the bushes, in the mountains and in the valleys seeking for a safe place to call home, the last place I wanted to be was in the zoo! One thing I dearly wanted was to sit back and cry. I wanted to grieve for my losses. I wanted to look back to my journey or stay awake and make sure it was not a dream. I was very exhausted mentally, physically, and spiritually.

Now it is very important to connect with a person in this kind of state, but no one had any idea of who I really was. I worked hard to fit in everyone's schedule while also attending to my family's needs in our new dream life! My children adjusted so fast and liked everything they were living, and my husband went from stress to depression. Life was too fast and stressful. I had only one option: to follow the flow.

I felt as if I was in a circus, and the language limitation did not help. I grew resentful. I felt violated again, but this time I must learn to like it. People around me were so loving and caring but they were missing something very crucial: I was a walking zombie. I was still bleeding emotionally. I was angry and hurting.

Life was spinning all around me. I felt dizzy and helpless. I searched deep within for something to which I could hold on. I found a very familiar feeling, "the fear of rejection," and grabbed it as a mighty savior. It became apparent to me that I could have time for everything except for prayer. I went to bed very late in the night and woke up early to resume those nonsensical activities.

There was an oppressing feeling in my spirit. For some reason, I felt restless and out of place. I realized that even though I was afraid of rejection from others, I responded to their goodness by resenting every good thing and the love shown to me.

I was given a second chance to start life over—a chance to lay down a new foundation, a broad horizon extended before me, but how can one do so, when there is no strength left to fetch from?

Coming to America was like being given an empty plot to build on. How and what do you build on it? It is up to each person, not even speaking of the choice of materials to use in building a new life.

Back then, there was a three-month period called "the honeymoon," where needs are met by the resettling agency and it's designed to help refugees recuperate from the hell they have gone through before starting over in a new life.

We spent the three months learning English. Driving was not new, but learning the traffic rules and regulations in America was terrifying. I will forever be thankful to the wonderful people who took time to help me adjust in this new life. These are people who do not need advertisements. I cherish each one in my heart. Many were for just that season, and a few stayed in my life and were used by the Lord to teach me the so-much-misunderstood unconditional love. These are precious hands the Lord used to disinfect my wounds—to compress my brokenness. To them,

I can't pay back. I can't thank them enough. I can only assure them I am aware that I couldn't get to where I am now without their obedience to the Lord to keep up with me.

During these three months called the honeymoon, we tasted a life that we never dreamed of. We visited places and people that we will never have access to, because of the prominent people who were around us.

Then the honeymoon period ended and we moved into an apartment. It was three days before Christmas in 2000. The apartment was vast— four bedrooms, two bathrooms, and a living and dining room. We even had our own laundry room. A certain church in Franklin gave me a car that belonged to a missionary who was out of the country for missions. I quickly read and memorized the driving instruction book. I drove around practicing with the many different people from the church who took turns to drive with me. Soon, I was driving a Ford Explorer on American streets. Oh my, my! Don't wake me up! It must be a sweet dream, I thought.

My first job in America was with the American Red Cross. I took a second shift, which started at 3:00 P.M. to 11:30 P.M. and most likely ended at 12:00 A.M., depending on the daily load. We processed blood, separating the red cells and platelets. I spent these 8-9 hours standing behind a centrifuge watching the packages of blood spinning. That was my sacred moment. I spent these precious hours with myself by myself because everyone assumed that I was not worthy of talking to. My supervisor handed me an assignment and instructions of what I was expected to do and would talk to me as loudly as he could to tell me to get him if I needed help. I never understood why people spoke to me shouting, as if I was deaf, until years later when I started my interpreting job.

I spoke to myself. I prayed to God. I had time to think through my life journey. In fact, this book came to me right there standing by the centrifuge. I wrote it on the table of my heart, hoping that one day I would be able to write it in English. Sometimes, tears would blind my eyes—tears of gratitude towards God's goodness. Sometimes, I would burst and chuckle—hiding my face in my white lab coat. I contemplated the wisdom of God and couldn't help vowing to say how He brought me through my troubles.

I was very proud and loved my job so much. I truly believe that the joy I experienced at that job was mostly because I spent those many hours by myself, sorting out things in my mind and spirit. Although at the end of my shift, my feet would have swollen, I was thankful to have a job in America and looking around me, all my coworkers were doing the same thing, so if they could do it, I knew I could do it too.

My first break lasted 15 minutes that was always around 5:30 P.M.   I would run to the phone and call my house to check on the girls, making sure they were doing their homework, giving them instruction on how to warm up food for dinner and take showers.   During my 30 minute break, which was around 9:30 P.M., I would talk to each one of my daughters and instruct the oldest to make sure they were in bed. As we spoke, I would ask her to make sure all the lights were out, and Dad's food was ready. I had her take CPR training when she turned 12 years old, at the Red Cross. Since I worked there, it was free for employees' families.

The girls were very understanding, and very proud of our new life. Everyone did what they were supposed to do.

Soon I learned a very life-changing lesson: the importance of "Time." I struggled to understand how come Time was money, but I learned quickly that Time is Life.

The length defining a day is a 24 hours which are given equally to everyone—to the president of United States of America, to the Pope, to the homeless guy under the bridge—we are all given the same amount of "time" each day. I felt so cheated by this thing called Time. It seemed as if the 24 hours in American culture were very much shorter than the African Time, which always seems stretchy.

The time here I am talking of is "chronos," which is a quantity of time that elapses. It is your 24 hours and mine. However you use it, will define your life and mine. That's why I said that, "Time is life."

Juggling a full time job and a full household's responsibility with a very real language barrier was a nightmare. I decided not to allow the new life to threaten me. I always fetched my strength from the memories of horrors and hell I lived through in Rwanda, Congo, and in Uganda.

I would come home late in the night, about 1:00 A.M. I would lie down for a few hours and be up to run by 6:00 A.M., getting the girls ready for school, then cleaning up and making meals, and doing laundry. Among the four of them, one would have a doctor's appointment, another would forget to take the school project, and I would have to take it to school. By the time everything was in place, it would be around 1:30 P.M. and time to get ready for work. This is how I fully embraced my new, crazy American life.

Through World Relief and the Government resettlement program, we were invited to participate in the American dream home owner program. We took the needed training. We also saved a certain amount of money, which was matched by the program, for a down payment, and we had our first home in America.

I heard someone say something about, "New levels, and new devils!" Believe me, this statement carries more truth than it sounds. While I was busy laying down the new foundation of our lives, little did I know that the enemy was busy doing what he does best. We are told that he comes to kill, steal, and destroy (John 10:10). The rest is a story to tell later.

I got invited to share my testimony in churches, schools, and homes. People were moved by the way the invisible, yet mighty, hand of God had protected me.

Soon, I realized that I was already ministering by sharing the power of God that sets men free.

I found it a necessity to learn the language and get training on how Christian work is done in the Western culture.

The moment I began thinking about stepping into my missionary calling, which was the whole purpose for my coming to America, then all hell broke loose.

It is important to emphasize that the enemy, Satan, gets alerted once he sees that one person has responded to the true call of God and is willing to embrace it. He doesn't bother himself with empty, bogus, and powerless people who just wake up to parade aimlessly. He actually makes sure they are kept busy doing nothing. I became a threat to him and his system, once I said, "Yes," to the Lord to use my brokenness to strengthen His people. I learned quickly that what threatens Satan is not how much we say we can do for God, it is how willing we are to be used by Him in His way and in His time. That willingness comes through prayer and meditating on the Word of God. This is a threat and Satan will do everything in his power to destroy anyone who has this potential.

Prayer used to be my number one hobby, and then when I came to America, I found it impossible to get my mind quiet enough to fellowship with the Lord. I got BUSY (BEING UNDER SATAN'S YOKE). One preacher defined it clearly.

Take my words for truth. This American dream is a trap of the enemy. It is a strategy and a yoke from hell to put and keep God's people in bondage. How many have succumbed!

Chasing after this dream has caused so many

of us to abandon basic life morals—the love of money, which is the root of all evil! The Apostle Paul warned the young Timothy and all of us in 1 Timothy chapter 6, saying that, "…Those who desire to be rich fall into temptation and a snare, and into many foolish and harmful lusts which drown men to destruction and perdition." There is sorrow that comes with this greediness. We humans have traded places with animals. We need little or no help from God almighty, the maker of everything. We have gone so far that we step on each other trying to get ahead and gain more to fulfill the American dream. Children are raised by television, while parents are working around the clock to get more money and get more stuff. The family life is soon to be a fairy tale that, "Once upon a time children sat down at a dinner table with Mom and Dad and spoke of how the day went by…"

Now do you see where I am going with this portion of my story? The family is the target of the enemy. Satan knows very well that if he can divide the family, he will have succeeded in his mission "to kill, steal, and destroy" so, the American dream is a bait. It is my opinion. You may disagree with me and all is well.

I am just sharing my journey and how I was affected each way up to where I am today.

In order to attract flies that were looming around your house, you would use honey to draw them together and then smash them altogether, isn't that right? How about a mouse that troubles your peaceful sleep? Don't you find bait that surely will get the job done with less mess to clean up afterwards? This is it! The bait has been strategically laid, and one after another we are succumbing. At no time in the history of America has there been such an outpouring of satanic influence as there is today. Pornography, murder, the movie industry, inspired by hell, is belching out all kinds of filthiness just for the sake of more money to capture the American dream! Watch out!

The Lord Jesus warned us about the god of this world—the one who rules the world's system. He said, "The prince of this world comes but it has found nothing in me." In II Corinthians 4:4 also, Paul noted how the god of this world blinded the eyes of those who have not believed, so that the light of the glorious gospel of Christ might not shine unto them. It is clear that Satan is the god of this world and is the one behind all the wicked principalities set up in high places to orchestrate the darkness and the wickedness on the earth, which are set up to oppose and deviate the will of God on earth and in the lives of God's people.

No servant can serve two masters; for he will love one and hate the other, or else he will hold to the one and despise the other. You cannot serve God and mammon. (Luke 16:13)

When mammon sits on the throne of one's life, he promises to offer the riches of the world in return for your worship. "If you bow down and worship me I will give you power, money and sex—these three are the reasons behind every transaction in today's business. Once you fall on your knees and happen to get one of the three, it comes with a list of what to do to keep it, which is usually costly as well. Mammon rules with fear. The threat of losing what you have causes many to work around the clock, keeping families apart, robbing them of the happiness of raising up Godly children, and at the end of the day, the choking truth is that when you pledged allegiance to mammon, he made it impossible to be satisfied, making you ungrateful and unable to appreciate God.

So many have lost families, dignity, health, and many souls are sold just to get some of the world's glory.

To illustrate this truth I would like to speak directly to you who are reading this chapter.

"Once upon a time there were troubles in one village—killings, famine, and all kind of calamities. One night, this loving family decided to escape, hoping to run as far as possible. They walked away from everything, carrying only their little ones. On the rough journey, they held the hope that there was a better life ahead. In the rain and in the sun they kept on, committed to get away from trouble. They arrived in a town. They saw that the city was built upon a high hill and was beautiful. The sun of that city never went down and the habitants were welcoming and nicer than anywhere else.

The couple pitched a tent, hoping to keep going once they could gain back strength. When they woke up in the morning, they found all kinds of gifts at their doorpost and the neighbors waiting to greet them. At the sight of all the stuff offered, the couple, without consulting each other, accepted the gifts and in amazement asked why were they well received since they were strangers! "It is our custom in this this town. We love guests, for we were all guests once," they responded. Where and how do you get all these nice things?

The next day they were taken to the king of the hill. They bowed down to him. They were told that if they stayed in the city, they would get prosperity, fame, and so on.

The king of the hill saw that the couple was not

in one accord about accepting the offer; he asked that the head of the household speak up.

On the way back, the wife said, "Honey, we are transiting. We should not take the gifts. You agreed without asking my opinion. This is not our final destination, remember?"

The man replied, "You must have lost your mind during this journey, if you think that we still have a better destination than this. I am tired of running. This is it. The offer is generous and also all the people here were also travelers and now, look, they are happy and settled."

The wife had a small note hand delivered by a woman who looked very old and tired for her age. There was no escape and inside the note was this sentence: "If you do not bow to the King, consider punishment: first time (hard work), second time (loss of what you got), third time (loss of what you brought with you), following times (shame and death). Signed by His excellency, Mammon."

She memorized the notice and destroyed the evidence. Fear grabbed her heart and the hope she once had was taken away.

One day, as her husband reported to worship the king of the hill, he was told that it had been noticed, "Your wife doesn't come to pay respect to the king." Before he could find another lie to tell, he was handed this notice: "If you do not bow to the King consider punishment: first time (hard work), second time (loss of what you got), third time (loss of what you brought with you), following times (shame and death)." Signed by His Excellency, Mammon.

He quickly kneeled down and worshipped as never before. He pledged his allegiance and promised the king to faithfully serve and honor him as long as he lived, but he was interrupted when he was reminded that when he spoke up the first time, "You spoke for the whole family. That being said, you must put order in your household. Everyone must bow down to the king. Otherwise, the punishment will be applied to you in the first place and then each one will get their share." He agreed and kissed the king. Then he went home.

With extreme rage, he addressed this "trouble-maker of a woman" without sharing the knowledge of the warning the notice signed by the king of the hill. They both kept it secret from each other. To be continued ……

Chapter Thirteen—The Wilderness

The wilderness is a place of trial where everything you know to be true is tested and the prince of the world administrates this test. Satan is he. It became clear that I had walked slowly into the wilderness.

The wilderness is one thing that nobody wants to hear about and no one wants to be in a wilderness because it is a place of loneliness and vulnerability.

Here, I want you to know that one can be lonely even in the midst of a room full of a hundred people. I came to understand that you could travel with someone without being together. On the same road, two can journey and have different experiences at the end of the road.

The wilderness is a testing place. The

wilderness is a dry place where the heavens are closed, the nights are dark and cold, and the days are hot, dry, and dusty. It is a place where nothing grows, and nothing survives except wild beasts.

Nobody wants to talk about the wilderness because it is not a pleasant place, therefore no manual books are written on what to do when you are in the wilderness. There are no clear instructions given to guide and warn travelers about this horrible place. However, the Word of God says something about one man who triumphed over this wilderness. Others are stories to tell. The man is Jesus Christ, our Lord and Savior.

"Now when all the people were baptized, it came to pass that Jesus also being baptized, and praying, the heaven was opened, And the Holy Ghost descended in a bodily shape like a dove upon Him, and a voice came from heaven which said, Thou art My beloved son; in Thee I am well pleased.

And Jesus being full of the Holy Ghost returned from Jordan, and was led by the Spirit into the wilderness, being forty days tempted of the devil. And in those days He did eat nothing: and when they were ended, He afterward hungered. And the devil, said to Him, if Thou be the Son of God, command this stone that it be made bread. And

Jesus answered him, saying, it is written, that man shall not live by bread alone, but by every word of God. And the devil, taking Him up into a high mountain, shewed unto Him all the kingdoms of the world in a moment of time. And the devil said unto Him, All this power will I give Thee, and the glory of them: for that is delivered unto me and to whomsoever I will I give it. If Thou therefore wilt worship me, all shall be Thine. And Jesus answered and said unto him, get thee behind Me, Satan: for it is written thou shalt worship the Lord thy God, and Him only shalt thou serve. And he brought Him to Jerusalem, and set Him on a pinnacle of the temple, and said unto Him, if Thou be the Son of God, cast Thyself down from hence: For it is written, He shall give His angels charge over Thee, to keep Thee: And in their hands they shall bear Thee up, lest at any time thou dash Thy food against a stone. And Jesus answering said unto him, it is said, Thou shalt not tempt the Lord thy God. And when the devil had ended all the temptation, he departed from Him for a season. And Jesus returned in the power of the Spirit into Galilee and there went out a fame of Him through the entire region round about. " (Luke 4:1-14)

I am forever grateful to the person of the Holy Spirit for the little knowledge I have today in the things of the Spirit, however, if I knew what I know today, when I was going into the darkest season of my life, I could have gone through it quickly and easily.

This season of my life became my high pinnacle—a position upon which I was able to see what the new life was offering and how to get it quickly.

As you may know, living in the American dream home comes with many obligations and these we were not aware of. The costs to up keep the dream and at the same time care for the normal life's responsibilities chained me down, which almost destroyed my faith and me, but it delayed the calling of God on my life. I worked hard to bring home my financial share. My husband had secured a daytime office job in this big company; how he got it I will never know. He made good money, dressed up nicely, drove a nice car and really lived his dream, while I moved from one job to another, trying to find a shift that could accommodate the needs of my four children. I worked in factories, in developmental homes and numerous nursing homes, all for the sake of keeping up with the dream life that I wasn't even living. I worked night shifts in order to attend to my children in daytime and the house chores. Then, the car that I was given by the church broke down. I was told that the cost to repair that car was higher than its actual price. It was pointless to get it fixed. My husband got me a brand new car and told me that I had to find money to pay for the car each month because there was no room for that car in the budget. I had no way to know the budget we had for he managed every coin that I made.

Soon, I had to find a weekend job because the money I was making was not enough. I found myself working seven days a week. I couldn't go to church anymore and this went on for years. With less sleep and much stress on my physical body, it caused me to almost double my weight. I gained 75 pounds during that period.

I almost lost my mind. When it became obvious that the more money we got, the more stuff he wanted, I made room in my hectic schedule to seek the Lord. I would use my break time and get on my knees in the bathroom or in my car. I fought to keep my eyes open every morning, sleeping behind the wheel. I cried to God for help as never before. I knew that there was no way to get out of this trap alive if the Lord didn't intervene on my behalf.

One day, I took a night off because I had to take care of one of my daughter's doctor's appointments during the day. I was exhausted. I couldn't do another shift. I used that day to fast and pray. I poured my heart out to God that day—a thing I hadn't done in years due to being BUSY (Being Under Satan's Yoke). I read the Word of God through the day and about the warfare of one who entangles himself with the affairs of this life, that he may please him who enlisted him as a soldier. Also, if anyone competes in athletics, he is not crowned unless he competes according to the rules. (II Timothy 2:4-5)

The following day, I reported to work as usual, on a night like other nights. In those nursing homes, there among the scriptures that my spirit was led to, was one which was troubling: "No one engaged in warfare entangles himself with the affairs of this life, that he may please him who enlisted him as a soldier." I tried to make sense of it and the more I tried, the more I got tangled. I didn't know how to untangle myself but He (God) did.

There were magazines and newspapers all over place. Anyone could pick whatever they wanted to look through in order to stay awake during the shift. Some watched television. As long as the work is being done in a timely manner, magazines and newspapers are tools to stay awake. I chose to read my Bible, seeking understanding of the above scripture because it really bothered my spirit. I knew then that there was no amount of money that I could make to satisfy that.

Then, the house supervisor sitting across the table watching TV told me that I shouldn't read the Bible at work. I asked what difference it made if one read the magazines or watched TV or stared in the air as long as the work was being done. We all thought it was a joke. The following night I came to work and was asked to sign administrative documents that I was being written up for reading the Bible while on the clock. I left and never went back. I didn't think that I was equipped to work under such an evil leader and with a team like that.

At home, my husband didn't want to know why I lost the weekend job. He made sure to remind me that we were both equally financially responsible. Each brings the share on a due date. I kept my full time job however.

In my Grandmother's house, we were taught to smile when we were hurting. We were told never to let self-pity define us. In spite of my aching heart, or perhaps because of it, I was kind of glad to have two days out of seven back. After all this time deprived of sleep, I needed to regain some rest, get the house together, and be with the girls again. I would rush home after my shift and by 7:45 A.M., if the traffic was light, I would find my oldest daughter home (she was still in middle school) getting ready to leave for school as well. I had taught her to help her sisters get ready, making sure each one dressed up in what I would have picked the night before. She raised her sisters while I was on a night shift all those years.

I cleaned, did laundry, and made meals before crashing on my knees before the Lord. I searched my heart to see what could be the reason for the unsettling feeling I had. There was no clear reason to me.

The pantry cleaned up quickly when it was not stocked. I dreaded to tell my husband that soon we would have no food, but inevitably I had to. I really needed no verbal answer from him. His facial expression said much more. I always expected:

"Have you asked your friends to help look for another weekend job?" He asked.

"Is this a question or a suggestion?" I boldly replied.

He said something about me being there every day instead of finding a second job.

I told him that I was praying for guidance and wisdom for the next step. He made a contemptuous face at me and passing me, he opened the pantry and shook his head and sat down to watch CNN as usual. I felt blood rushing to my head. I responded with so much anger that I should have regretted it later, but it revealed to me something I couldn't have known if I hadn't pushed the button in that area.

"Can't you be happy for me that I am able to sleep two nights in the house? I have worked two jobs for the entire time we have been in this house and...." Before I could finish the sentence, he said:

"Wait until they take your car away. Then you will pray more. "

"You mean you can't pay for my car note with the income we have?"

The conversation revealed that I was trapped and the so-much-needed car was a bet.

I needed the car to get to work and this was the only transportation we (the girls and I) had. This was a threat!

I begged him to find "room in the budget" as he always said, for my car. We argued and screamed at each other like never before. I reminded him that anytime we presented him with our needs, there was always no money, so I asked him to tell me what was in the budget that made it saturated if there was no room for our priorities! He became so angry, so abusive physically; emotionally this was like pinching my old wounds.

I wish I could tell you that God told me to quit my weekend job. I wish I could say that I heard a strong conviction that it was the will of God, because that could make sense and strengthen my faith, but the truth is that the anger against the injustice done to me all the way up to that time made me realize that no one would stand for me if I couldn't stand up for myself.

The Supervisor called me and told me that they appreciated my work and were asking me to come back and cover my shift as long as I would not read the Bible at work.

It is never easy to make the right decision. Going back to that job was the right thing to do. It could change the entire atmosphere in my home. It could spare my car; bring food and peace in my home again. I, however, declined the offer for reasons I didn't understand then.

A time came when a benevolent and capable friend convinced me to enroll in the Nursing program; her family would pay for the whole four years.

I lacked family support. There was no way I could keep a full time job and be a fulltime student in the nursing program and at the same time fully take care of a family of six. I was really stuck!

Perhaps you can relate to this concept: "Being

stuck, threatened, abandoned, helpless and so on…"

I chose to recount this period of my life through this chapter and called it the wilderness, because I wanted to bring home to you the concept of wilderness.

The wilderness is God's refining place for everyone who will ever become anything in His hands. There, alone, we are faced with major decisions to make.   There, alone, my fear of poverty and rejection pushed me to my knees. My desires and motives were weighed. I dug deep down in my faith to see what could sustain me and found nothing.

Many people think that our destiny has nothing to do with our daily decision-making—that we just walk in it as we go. In the book you are reading, pay attention and you will see how one's destiny can be deviated and delayed. Again, the message I am bringing is of redemption and of restoration, but no one walks into it just like that. There is a cost to pay. There is a price to pay in every decision you will make.

Once you find your life on a lonely path and on a lowly key, once you discover that your heart and mind are disconnected, and your vision is dimmed to the point where you start moving into strange paths, be careful!   The devil may be around the corner to try you out.

My wilderness was a testing ground. When soldiers are practicing to shoot, they are carried into the bush where arbitrary targets are set. There, they will learn how to distinguish voices and tricks of the enemy. Sometimes, soldiers are blindfolded to train their instincts and teach them how to trust them. This is a place where your emotional, physical, and spiritual abilities are checked out, because it is not on the battlefield you teach a man how to shoot or aim at an enemy. It is not on the battlefield that you check out how long you can hold your breath while hiding from the enemy.

This season brought back all the old, familiar feelings; the old scars became wounds again. Here, I was on foreign soil in the great America, but haunted by the same old demons. I crawled every surface of my house crying to God for help as usual. I prayed and fasted in my old victim mind- set attitude and nothing happened.

My wilderness was a challenge to change or to remain the same. The power to change and a way to go about it I had not. The fear to remain the same paralyzed me.

Somehow during that "seeking God" period, I got clarity of mind. I saw that though I was haunted by the same devils of the past, I, this time, had the power to decide about how I would rebuild my life on this soil. However, the cost was great!

Perhaps you've had a friend who was simultaneously your best friend and your worst enemy. I had one! When he was pleased, I walked on the clouds, but hell was my back yard when I didn't meet his expectations.

It became clear to me that there was no way I could shift from the "victim" mentality and embrace a change so great as to become all that God wanted me to be without going through the wilderness. It was as if God was saying to me, "I love you too much to leave you halfway." I walked with God at the helm through a new land with new people and languages. My wilderness was a summary of events and situations I had gone through before. It was a final review before I could graduate from fear of rejection, inadequacy, and self-pity. It was intense! When I refused to work a second job to enter my missionary work, the extra income that brought us food and other feminine products was cut off. My husband stood firm in his decision that if I could not make that money, he wasn't going to give up anything.

One day I met a young woman. She was a coworker of my husband. I shared with her my struggle to find a church like the one in which I grew up. She told me about the church where she attended and asked if I could visit one Sunday. In 2002, one Sunday I visited New Song Fellowship Church in the Cool Springs area, with Pastor Dale Evrist. One thing led to another. I was enrolled in their school of ministry, which laid a solid foundation for the journey I embarked on in America. (I made a decision that was a serious prayer that led to a serious challenge—speak about the beginning of the ministry). I learned the foundation of Christian ministry. My vision became more clear and confirmed.

Let's look into the account of Jesus in the wilderness.

"... And the devil said unto Him, if Thou be the Son of God, command this stone that it be made bread." (Luke 3) Think about this. Satan knew well that Jesus would multiply bread and feed thousands sometime in His lifetime, so he (Satan) took advantage of His (Jesus') present need and weakness to convince Him to use His power out of season and for a wrong reason.

In October, 2003, I invited African Christian leaders from different States in America and abroad to come. We gathered in Nashville, Tennessee, where I reside. The New Song Fellowship Church sent me a worship team led by

John Hall, who was by that time the pastor of outreach missions.

I stood before them on Friday night, Saturday, and Sunday. I poured out my heart to them. This is what people call "casting the vision." Deep in my heart, I believed I was ready and this was the time and the reason was right.

I learned during this season that there must be a waiting period, which involves watering and pruning for a planted tree to bring forth fruits. I was newly planted. The vision and passion to serve the Lord was burning ardently. Then, I violated the process and set out to do the work that I was not fully equipped to do—helping people who didn't need my help yet. The little money that came for this cause brought strife into my home. As you may remember when I resigned my second job, we were short of that amount of money which caused so much fighting. Every little bit of money that came for the ministry was snatched from my hands and used for daily needs. The ministry grew, however, and from the outside, things looked fine. I travelled and ministered from church to church across the country and abroad.

It was during this season, that I was convicted about failing the temptation to make bread from stones. I failed the test. When I was offered the opportunity to deny my faith and devotion in the Word of God, I overcame the temptation. When I was offered the opportunity to bow down and forsake my calling to the best of getting an education that could set me and my girls up financially, I overcame, and the devil left for the opportune time. How I pray for you that you will be able to recognize that opportune time! When after you have overcome a number of temptations and he (the devil) comes back in a different suit, may he find you vigilant. So, "Watch and pray, lest you enter into temptation." I got busy and didn't see him coming back; therefore, I wasn't vigilant. I failed so badly.

In October, 2005, we held our last convention. At this point, the African Global Mission had grown, and I was being recognized, which felt so good!

Dr. Moses Wang Lee from South Korea, who resided in Atlanta, Georgia, was one of our guest speakers. He stood up and praised the work that "this young woman" was doing and asked me, before the entire audience, to get my travel documents ready because he was taking me to South Korea to raise funds that would help run the ministry.

For a while I had forgotten about adversity. I was on my way to success! Dr. Wang Lee made me a target for destruction. Everyone turned against me. They all ran after the Korean man who caused much division in their midst as well. It seemed that it was the end of me and the work of the African Global Mission.

For years, I was left behind and forsaken. On my knees seeking for understanding of what had just happened, I was granted so much grace to see that the call of God in my life was genuine and irrevocable, but the time was not right. With fear and trembling, I decided to put the ministry of the African Global Mission on hold.

My wilderness got prolonged. You see, in many cases, when you fail the examination you are given two choices, to quit or to retake the test. I chose to retake the test, and was committed to pay whatever the cost would be to gain the victory over any area of my life that the Lord was not pleased with.

Little did I know what the cost would be!

I enrolled in a Master's program at the Newburgh Theological Seminary and College of the Bible, and did most of my work on line and on weekends while attending to my family and a fulltime job.

With the help of the people I met during my ministry, my seminary education was paid and in the same way the great needs I faced daily were provided for, because even in the wilderness, He, "the Lord," makes an oasis just for whosoever wills to obey.

I can still hear the skeptical voices of discouragement coming from the most trusted people now; "You mean you will not move with the ministry until you hear from God?" You are wasted and a pain to the family.

I remember well those nights spent on my knees, when my head was spinning due to physical and mental fatigue. It is easy to fight the outside enemy and come home to be comforted and rest to regain strength for the next round, but it is another story when you do not have a home-life support system to retire to.

I truly believe that this situation wasn't strange to the great apostles and others who dared to choose the way of the wilderness—the narrow door.

"We are hard-pressed on every side, yet not crushed; we are perplexed, but not in despair; persecuted, but not forsaken; struck down, but not destroyed"

(II Corinthians 4: 8-9)

Months turned into years. Still, I had no desire to go back to the ministry. I only felt the need to lay low as if an invisible, heavy hand had grabbed my neck and pressed me down. Down there I waited.

I devoured the Word of God; I fed on it. I slept on it. I recited scriptures back to God. I reminded Him of the promises He made to "whosoever will." I became like a mad woman. The funny side of this period of my testimony is that God would lead someone who greatly needed a prayer to me and in obedience I would suck up my pain, and then minister to God's precious people as He allowed me. He used me to patch together marriages that were under attack while mine was failing gradually. He used me to bring clarity in ideas to those who were struggling to begin their ministries, while I was put on the shelf.

It was during this season that I reached out to support a group of women survivors of the genocide war in Rwanda. Just to encourage my weary spirit, or maybe to check my motives, He would open a small window for me to serve.

He would make a way out of nowhere just to confirm His faithfulness to me. Such memories shake my heart to the core, bringing me to my knees. A few months before the completion of my Ph.D., I was not able to meet the financial requirements and the only option I had was to quit. In my desperation, pleading for the Lord to make a way for me, He surely did! I received a phone call from a young woman whom I always considered like a young sister. Her husband was a young lawyer whose heart is of gold. She invited me to her house but I couldn't go because I didn't have enough fuel to drive across the city, so she settled her little boys in the car and came to my house. She handed me an envelope and told me to wait and not open it until she left. When I opened it, there was a check for $2,100.00 folded in a thank you card from her husband. I knew then that only the Living God could move in such a way as this. This money was enough to assure the school that I was truly committed, so they would make a payment plan for the remaining amount. I called the couple to thank them without saying what the money was going to be used for since they didn't need to know anyway.

A few days later, the same young woman called me again and told me that she had something for me from her father-in-law who was a lawyer as well. This time, I drove there and there was another check for $1,500.00! The total paid off the money I owed the seminary and paid for my gown, cap, and regalia. I shared the victory with my husband and children. The girls were very happy and proud of me, but their father was so displeased and I couldn't figure out the reason. I heard someone saying that the night gets darker before the dawn of the morning; I can't find enough words to agree more with this notion. I can only tell you that I was navigating from one challenge to another. I would get knocked down and then get up shaking off the dust to get knocked down again.

I settled down for a while to work on my dissertation, full of hope and gratitude toward the Lord for paying the debt I owed the school. This was a great victory; I could dream again. I began seeing the end of the tunnel.

What I didn't know was that the mortgage hadn't been paid for months. The final notice from the mortgage company was left on the kitchen counter unopened. The red seal on the envelope was alarming so I opened the envelope. We were being informed that our mortgage delinquency had reached $7,300.00; we were not allowed to make any payment arrangement unless we paid the above amount in full. We were given 21 days to respond.

I wondered how to approach my husband since he hasn't said much. For a while, he was in and out the house, just like a bad roommate. I called him asking what had happened and what were we going to do in 21 days? I was told to, "Figure it out since I was a Ph.D. candidate; that I received money, hid it, and used it for my selfish needs." I was accused. I picked up the phone and called the mortgage company apologizing hysterically.

I stood there with my heart pounding and my legs shaking as I spoke with the mortgage agent who told me that we owed three months with late fees and all applied penalties, and hadn't been responding to their calls. I have felt hopelessness to the point where I wanted to end my life; this was one of those dark moments when all become dark, when nothing made sense. I couldn't think of finding a job in 21 days, and even if I could, I was not going to get $7,300.00 at once. I was going to give up on my studies; forget the final dissertation. I was completely defeated. I felt forsaken by God. I crawled on my knees in agony for 14 days holding the final notice in my hands. I had reached the end of diplomacy.

Religiously, we pray, with well-arranged sentences and calmed voices because we have been told that in the presence of the most-high God we are standing in awe. I violated all the religious protocols. I crawled every corner of my house. I almost lost my mind at this point. I just kept repeating, "You must do something about this. There must be a way out of this, and there must be an answer. You have to do something, Lord."

I am thankful to the person of the Holy Spirit

who is able to intercede for us in our weakness when I couldn't find words to say. When I didn't know what and how to pray, He prayed for me.

Prior to those days I had spoken to a Women's ministry at Smyrna First Baptist Church on Mother's Day of 2006. There, I met a sweet woman who had a book store. She promised to get me all the books I needed to prepare for my Ph.D. dissertation. One afternoon, I received a call from the church secretary to tell me that there was a box with my name on it delivered to that church and that I should come to get it, so I did. She asked me if there was anything she could do for me (as you know, this is a courtesy formula). I heard myself saying out of nowhere, "I need an appointment with the senior pastor."

"What is the reason for the appointment?" she asked.

I heard myself again saying, "It's a personal matter."

"Do you want him alone or his wife along?"

I replied, "Yes, both."

We met at Starbucks in Smyrna. Pastor Pat Hood and his sweet wife, Amy, were across the table. Not much introduction was needed, since Amy was at the Mother's Day celebration the day I was invited to speak. She surely remembered me and was excited to see me again. He asked what we needed to talk about. I struggled to articulate. I murmured something about being in trouble with the mortgage because I didn't make enough money to complete my financial dues in the family. I handed him the final notice, which was no longer legible because it was wrinkled and stained by tears. They both stared at this letter and said something to each other. Then, they said, "I think we can do this."

The rest is a beautiful story of God's faithfulness. He made a way again! He broke the yoke off my neck again! Praise the Lord for His mercy over me.

Dr. Brigitte Kitenge Doctorate Graduation Class of 2007

Dr. Kitenge with Dr. Glen Molette, President of Newburgh Theological Seminary, Indiana, USA (Pictured Right) 2007

Chapter Fourteen: A Painful Lesson—Forgiveness

" It took me some 44 years to get to this junction. I must own it or I will be forever a victim," I heard myself saying.

About two years had gone by, since my husband had left us. The day came. I got a phone call from my lawyer telling me that his lawyer requested that he be allowed to come home to get his stuff. It was an order and I must be present.

What a torture! He chose to come that Saturday morning. I had just finished a night shift. I was tired and I had to go back to work that same evening. He went corner-by-corner, drawer-by-drawer, like a tornado. He was apparently angry and I understood! I was in the bed the entire time pretending not to care. I was angry with God and with this man to whom I gave twenty-six years of my life, and I was also angry with myself for being me.

My two youngest daughters came in to keep me company. They sat in my king-sized bed just so I could sleep. I took a sleeping pill to knock the pain out, but before it could take effect, a window was opened in my memory to a dream I had had years ago. In that dream, my husband was packing his things and leaving me; he was angry, screaming, and breaking things in the house. What a deja vue! With the exception of the screaming, the dream was live before my eyes. I closed my eyes and silently cried myself to sleep.

Throughout the night shift's work, I couldn't dismiss the dream I had had some twenty years ago. Did God warn me about the man I chose to marry? If yes, then I missed the warning and I was reaping the fruits of my disobedience.

During my ministry as a hospital chaplain I met several people who were extremely mad at God because of the adversity that had come their way. I felt connected with people in great pain. They lay alone, moaning in anguish. I could, in many ways, empathize with their suffering, but anything I tried to say, seemed so weak and stiff, as if it was memorized from a pastoral care manual.

How I wanted to be real—to share with them my heart and my experience with pain!

One day, not long after my divorce, I visited a patient who was on a suicidal watch, and as usual, I followed the hospital pastoral care guide. I sat there and listened to this man, who at 53 years old, had decided to end what he called a useless life by setting himself on fire. His whole body was wrapped up; I could only see his eyes, nose, and a hole where his mouth supposedly was. It took me three visits to get him to open up to me. His voice was weak and echoed anger and maybe regret. I asked him if I could sit. He nodded. For about fifteen minutes I sat there. The room was extremely hot and smelled strongly of disinfectant. John was heavily sedated. He was not lucid, and he was in and out of consciousness. He asked me why I kept coming. "What do you really want from me?"

I told him that I just wanted to hear his voice. He slowly turned away from me, asking where did my accent come from. I told him that I was from Rwanda. Then he turned back toward me with a groaning of pain in his voice. He asked me how I got here (in America). I told him to make a deal; if he told me how he got there (in the hospital bed), I would tell him how I got to America.

Listening to his story brought back to my memory my own story. His story was so familiar, I could finish each sentence of his tale. You never know how much you really believe anything until its truth or falsehood becomes a matter of life and death to you. I came to realize that John, and many others still believing that God is in control of every situation, also believed He can be blamed when things go wrong. So many believe that marriage is "till death do them part," so they can help death to occur when life together doesn't fit their expectations.

God again, "Please don't tell me anything about God."

"Forgive him? Are you serious? After what he has done to me? I can never forgive him!"

"Forgive me? How can God forgive me? You don't know what I have done. How could I have done such an awful thing? I can't forgive myself."

These are some of many confessions I have heard every day as a minister—confessions from people who have grown up in church, in Christian homes—yet grown up without fully understanding God's forgiveness and its intended effect on every level of life.

Writing this chapter prompted me to reflect back on the many years of torments, nightmare-filled dreams, waking up sweating, haunted by images of people and events that had shattered my life. The inability to release them from my memory kept me a prisoner of hatred.

One of the most frustrating things I had to endure is that God was oftentimes so quiet, that when I had finished pouring out my heart to the Lord, I would like a little response—a word of comfort—anything to help me hang on, but He was silent. Then, I reached a conclusion that: Maybe there is no God, or maybe He is not interested in me. His silence made adversity much more difficult to endure, because the view of God as a loving and caring father was compromised by His silence. Soon, the blame game changed when blaming God didn't ease my pain, but still I couldn't get over the fact that the loving God kept silent when I cried to Him for help and comfort. In my view, I saw that when God rejected me, He gave my enemy the right to abuse me.

When John told me that he couldn't forgive God and the wife who abandoned him when he most needed help, it was a dejà vue episode of my own story.

Forgiveness is a very crucial process; it is an act of the will. It really requires a full understanding of one's need to be forgiven. Once we understand the depth of our sin and the distance it put between God and us, and once we get a glimpse of the sacrifice God made to restore fellowship with us, we should not hesitate to need the process of forgiveness. I dreaded this process, because of the vulnerability it imposed on me. I made a retrospective visit of my journey and didn't like what I was seeing; I was reminded of times when I doubted God's love and care for me. I could remember places that I reached where I felt so alone and I questioned His presence that was promised to me through His Word. I was convicted of my foolishness of having thought that I made it when numerous people didn't make it. The fear of God fell on me when I realized how many times I could have been killed. I thought of the many attacks and assaults that could have completely destroyed me, and how many times I was given back my life even when I attempted to take it myself. When this process is ignored; walls of hatred and bitterness are built and one's life is trapped. The lack of forgiveness, which is no forgiveness, leads to bondage, which is the root of many problems in one's life.

Peter came to Jesus and said to Him, "Lord,

how often shall my brother sin against me, and I forgive him?" He asked a question and Jesus answered, but to many of us the question is not how many times we should forgive the person who sins against us. It is one thing to forgive someone who acknowledges the wrong they did and apologizes somehow for it, but how do we forgive a heartless individual who feels no remorse nor pity for his victims? In my case, I had turned my other cheek so many times that my cheekbones were tenderized and I no longer agreed with the scripture in Matthew 5: 39. "But I say not to resist an evil person. But whoever slaps you on your right cheek, turn the other to him also." I don't like this. It makes me sick. It is the only scripture I disagree with because I still don't understand it. Nowadays, we are seeing sick minds and evil doers hiding behind insanity. You can turn your other cheek if you want to. I have seen evil doers, heartless people, and made up my mind. If I can't stand my ground to protect myself, I will take off running for my life—no more turning the other cheek.

This is a slap in the face of anyone who has been a victim of abuse and injustice. It has been used as a religious tool to keep weak victims in the shadows. I am sure it has a more spiritual sense, but it has been misinterpreted and many have been hurt. So, for my fellows who are dealing with the question; how many times must one forgive the individuals who continuously seek to destroy your life, who heartlessly stop at nothing until they are satisfied by the destructions done, I pray that God gives you directions on how to escape that evil.

Think of an eight year-old little girl who is sold into sex slavery—whose innocence is taken every time she regains her strength from the previous abuser. Just for a minute, have that picture in your mind if you can? My conclusion on the subject of forgiveness is that forgiveness is a painful process and no one can mentor nor teach about it. We cannot talk about it enough. There are several steps to a successful forgiveness process. It is a genuine work of God through the power of the Holy Spirit in one's life that convicts us of our own sinful nature and evil doings which produces the need to be forgiven.

The story of the sinful woman and the tale of two debtors in Luke 7 would help me bring a conclusion to this section of my journey that was so very painful that it kept this book in the drawer for years.

A woman who was known in the whole city for her sinful life style approached the Lord Jesus humbly and fearfully crying for her condition. It would be hard for some of you to understand the scenario if you haven't been publically humiliated or associated with a shameful event. Just for a minute, picture some 12 or more pairs of judging eyes all turned toward this strange woman. The Bible tells that she stood at His feet behind Him weeping; and she began to wash His feet with her tears and wipe them with the hair of her head. She kissed His feet and anointed them with the fragrant oil.

In order to shed enough tears to wash a man's feet, and bend over to the ground until your face is right in the dust to have your hair close enough to wipe the feet, you must have been arrested and convicted by the power of the Holy Spirit. In order to help them understand this concept, the Lord gave imagery about two debtors and the conclusion is; to whom much is given, much is required.

Only when we are aware of our need for forgiveness, seek that forgiveness, and accept it, are we then able to offer forgiveness to those who have offended us. You cannot give what you don't have, and no one can lead to a place they haven't been. The scriptures tell us that it is the goodness of God that brings sinners to repentance. I couldn't agree more.

1 Have mercy on me, O God,
According to your unfailing love;
according to your great compassion
blot out my transgressions.
2 Wash away all my iniquity
and cleanse me from my sin.
3 For I know my transgressions,
and my sin is always before me.
4Against you, you only, have I sinned
and done what is evil in your sight;
so you are right in your verdict
and justified when you judge.
5Surely I was sinful at birth,
sinful from the time my mother conceived
me
6 Yet you desired faithfulness even in the
womb;
you taught me wisdom in that secret place.
7 Cleanse me with hyssop, and I will be
clean; wash me, and I will be whiter than
snow.
8 Let me hear joy and gladness;
let the bones you have crushed rejoice.
9 Hide your face from my sins
and blot out all my iniquity.
10 Create in me a pure heart, O God,
and renew a steadfast spirit within me.
11 Do not cast me from your presence

or take your Holy Spirit from me.
12 Restore to me the joy of your salvation
And grant me a willing spirit, to sustain me.
13 Then I will teach transgressors your ways,
So that sinners will turn back to you.
(Psalm 51)

The 13th verse speaks of the point I am trying to bring to your attention. You cannot forgive unless you have fully accepted God's forgiveness and restoration.

How I pray that the true teacher, the one who is capable of convicting the greatest sinner to repent, might cause you to cry over your condition like David in Psalm 51.

Chapter Fifteen—Touch My Scars

We cannot talk about scars without talking of wounds, because scars originate from wounds.

The Merriam dictionary defines a wound as: an injury to the body (as from violence, accident, or surgery) that typically involves laceration or breaking of a membrane (such as the skin) and usually damage to underlying tissues or a mental or emotional hurt or blow. Here we will focus on emotional wounds rather than physical ones. They are hidden; no one sees or feels them except the owner of them. Emotional wounds are hard to heal and because they are hidden, they often get infected and the infection contaminates one's behavior. Some wounds are painful and harder to heal than others—such as a wound caused by loved ones or close friends. The same offense committed by a distant acquaintance and one committed by a family member or a close friend are different, to the point that one can easily be dismissed by just ignoring and avoiding the offender, but the wound caused by a family member hurts deeply and takes time to heal.

I heard the story of a man by the name of Joseph, the son of Jacob, sharing his dream with his half-brothers which caused him to be thrown into a pit and later on sold into slavery. One thing led to another and he found himself in prison in a strange country. This man knew what rejection meant. Hatred and betrayal were not new vocabularies to him. No one knows how long the journey toward Egypt lasted, how long he served in Potiphar's palace, or how long he was in prison. The young man, whose father made a robe of many colors, was stripped naked, and out of the pit he became a slave on strange soil in an unknown language and culture. I can easily relate to this experience because I know how It feels to be uprooted and leave all that you have ever known behind—learning a new language and struggling to understand the culture and make a living in a hostile environment. Many people see Joseph as evidence of how God can lift one up from prison to the palace. This is completely true, but few people understand the daily struggles he overcame; the anguish, the fear, the shame and the injustice. All these were caused by what his own brothers decided to do because of the hatred and jealousy they had against him.

During the couple of visits I paid to John in the hospital burn unit, I saw a wounded person. He was literally wounded physically and in his soul as well. It is hard—almost impossible—for a person like John to heal because of the source of his wounds. The rejection in his childhood by his mother and her boyfriend, the abuse by his manipulative, alcoholic grandmother, the divorce and loss of all his wealth, his dignity, and to worsen the story, his attempt to kill himself with fire were overwhelming. John is one among the many cases that made me quit the hospital chaplaincy. I knew what to do to cast out depressing spirits and liberate the captives, but I was bound by the hospital policies. So many things in life can wound one's heart, break and crush one's spirit, but in my experience, the most traumatic event that almost completely destroyed me in my adult and Christian life was the divorce.

I have endured many adversities in the past. I wear marks and scars that prove what I went through. In 1996, after enduring the pain caused by the genocide of the Rwandan Tutsi tribe, I fled to Zaire where my husband was from, hoping to completely recover from my many losses and one day live a normal and maybe a happy life again. I knew that I wasn't the ideal wife in the family, but the season changed and I was unwanted and unwelcome—unfitting in my husband's circle.

It is difficult to go on living in a hostile environment. It is impossible to carry on, knowing that the only person you trusted with everything left to live for, was planning to get another woman. It took me years to heal from the emotional wound left on my soul by that event. I was pregnant and had a craving for bananas and peanuts. I went into my husband's working shoulder bag. Instead of money, I found love letters and pictures of Micheline—the woman soon to replace me. My spirit was crushed, my heart broke into pieces; that day every effort I made to keep going became vain.

I will always remember the day I confronted him about the issue, He called his family members who were living with us and that night they confronted me. Theo, the "money changer," came with empty bottles of beer and a false witness. I have never drunk alcohol. My husband knew it, but he didn't stand up for me. The charge was made that I brought men home when no one was there. (They all knew that there was always someone home, so much went on.) She did this, she said that--just accusation after accusation. These were big offenses culturally. They were trying to find ways to send me out. I felt alone and betrayed. This event wounded my soul. These are wounds I am trying to help you identify, because what is revealed can be dealt with. If it is hidden, it will rot and get infected.

I told you the story of Joseph, the son of Jacob, a man who knew sorrow, a man who was deeply wounded. He could have been stuck in a mental prison because of the pain he endured for those many years, but he chose to see God's hand through it all, therefore, he was able to say, "As for you, you meant evil against me; but God meant it for good, in order to bring it about as it is this day to save many people alive." (Genesis 50:20) He called his first son, Manasseh, saying, "for God has made me forget all my toil and my father's entire house." He named the second son, Ephraim, "for God has made me fruitful in the land of my affliction." Only a healed soul can see good out of evil. Only the restoring hand of the Lord can open a blind person's eyes to see fruitfulness where pain and sorrow, injustice and betrayal once dwelt. It is only God's grace that makes one forget the toil of the past. I chose to see good out of every evil that I endured.

The Oxford English dictionary defines a scar as: A mark left on the skin or within body tissue where a wound, burn, or sore has not healed completely and fibrous connective tissue has developed. Or
a lasting effect of grief, fear, or other emotion left on a person's character by an unpleasant experience.

Yes, I was wounded both physically and emotionally. It really hurt so badly that I learned never to remember the people who wounded my heart. I clung to the one who heals wounded hearts, therefore, I can see God's grace springing out of my scars.

Only a healed soul can sing "Amazing grace, how sweet the sound that saved a wrench like me. I was once lost, but now I'm found, was blind but now I see." When I was about to write this chapter, I felt compelled to meet with my ex-husband. I battled the idea for weeks and I felt uneasy. There was a weight on my heart and every time I pushed the thought off. In the night, I had a series of dreams and nightmares. I knew then that I needed to act on the thoughts of meeting him. I went on my knees and prayed for clarity. You may wonder, "Did you really have to pray to meet your ex?" Yes, dear one, I did. Unless you know what an investment I made in this marriage and what the divorce took from me, then you wouldn't understand why I needed to make sure I was hearing from the Lord.

I sent him a text requesting a phone call. He agreed after a series of questions. We met in my new home. It felt as if I were in labor the entire 36 hours before that meeting. It lasted an eternity. I wanted it done, once and for all. In the past when I attempted to make peace, the efforts were not appreciated and the results were always chaotic. I rehearsed my three points that I needed to talk about, making sure my heart and mind were in tune.

All the lights were on in the living room, I wanted to be able to make eye contact with him, which he had avoided since the day he left the house. I made spiced tea and then sat down. He asked me in a nonchalant manner what I called him for. I struggled to keep "Brigitte" out of this meeting, because everything in me wanted to respond in the same manner. I mumbled, "Lord Jesus, help me," and then I began.

"Daddy, I have three things I must tell you. You do not have to respond. I just ask you to listen. There is no need to argue. You don't even have to agree with me. If you have anything to say in response to what I am about to tell you, please let us meet again on your terms."

"I would like to thank you for many things. If only I could number them one by one, but since the human memory is corrupted, allow me to summarize the 26 years of our life together—the many good moments we shared, the long journey we took together, the four daughters we raised, the many ends and new beginnings we experienced together—all are to be cherished deep in my heart. The hard times and bad decisions that ended our marriage made me strong, so please understand that I am thankful for each step we took together."

He was so uncomfortable, he couldn't stay still, and still there was no eye contact, no matter how close I was. He asked me why I was doing this. I told him that at the end, he would understand why.

"Daddy," I said, "you may not be where you can forgive me yet, but I would like you to know that I take 100% responsibility for the failure of our marriage. I free you from any and all heartbreaks that we both experienced that caused us to blame each other. If you can receive forgiveness, please receive mine. You have given me so much; you have taught me to be tough. When you were not there and I had nowhere to turn, the mighty hand of God reached down and grabbed me. In His wisdom, He comforted me. He brought healing and hope to me. Therefore, I am extending the goodness of God to you. I truly pray and hope that you will one day be able to surrender your life to the Lord Jesus, receive forgiveness, and learn to forgive. Until then, please reconcile with the girls. You and I are divorced, but you will never divorce them. They are innocent victims of our mistakes. They are your children and nothing will change that."

There were some tears and a long silence. I asked him if I could pray and he agreed. There were more tears and sobbing. I asked him why he was crying and he said, "I am not strong like you."

Strong is how it should feel when you nip in the old wounds. I knew that I was healed. When the chains that once kept you captive lie at your feet, when you stand tall before what used make you tremble, then you know healing has taken place. I uncovered my wounds that day; I pinched them. There was neither blood coming out nor pus. I am healed; my scars are beautifully firm. Out of them springs God's grace.

Uncovered wounds produce ugly scars. A wound marks an event, and a scar relates that event. It tells the story. Scars speak of what, when, and how it happened. What's the story told by your scars?

Chapter Sixteen—Hope Again

The World estimated a million people were killed during those roughly 100 days during the Rwandan holocaust, but to me it is more.

I wish I could tell you what I went through day by day, but a testimony is no good if it can't uplift the hearer. I spent the following seven years on the run seeking for a safe place to raise my children. I went from Rwanda to Congo, from Congo to Uganda, and from Uganda to the USA in 2000.

During those many years on the road to safety, I experienced so much pain, suffering, and injustice. I was abused beyond explanation; I was victimized to my last human value. I lost many family members. I lost my dream, my dignity, and I lost HOPE.

I became a prisoner of hatred and anger. I was angry at everyone, including GOD. I woke up each morning and fed myself with more hatred and more anger. This became my passion; I rehearsed my misery every day and became a well-done victim.

I was lost in darkness, and soon I found myself in bondage. The weight of broken dreams, the loss of my dignity, the loneliness—all this created emptiness in my heart that made it impossible to see anything good coming my way. Step by step, I became depressed and could not see any way out. Then, I attempted to kill myself. I threw myself in the Lake, Lake Kivu, for those who know the region.

The night before killing myself, in my depression, I told myself:

"I can't take it anymore!
My burden too heavy to carry,
I am lost in the dark,
I am empty and dry,
I have no strength to cry,
My heart is too heavy to lift,
Death has its power over me
Who will deliver me?"

I walked away from my children, knowing that I would never see them again. I dragged my feet all the way to the lake carrying the pain and the guilt, the failure of not being able to feed and protect my children, and ending my life was the only way to ease this torture (I thought).

This was my turning point! When they fished me out of the water, I stayed in a coma for days and meanwhile, the Lord was doing a work on my heart.

On the road to recovery from my suicidal scandal, shame and failure, I had one desire: to know God and the power of His love. This desire introduced Hope into my life. My situation as a refugee in Congo and in Uganda did not change. What changed was the way I saw my journey and everything I went through so far.

My dear friends, when I look into people's eyes, I can only imagine the pain they have experienced during their journey. Though our stories may be different and our circumstances or languages may be different, there is one thing we have in common: we all know what it means to hurt.

Suffering is a universal language; tears are the same for Asians or Africans, for Muslims and for Christians, for white and for black or brown.

I am not saying that I am a hero. I am here

because grace and mercy found me. My loss, my failure, my pain and fear were lifted, HOPE and HEALING took place.

Webster's dictionary defines Hope as: Desire accompanied by expectation of belief in fulfillment, to hope is to desire with expectation of obtainment.

When Hope was born in my heart, I could see a better tomorrow for my girls and myself. Through the eyes of Hope, I saw myself standing in America sharing the testimony of God's faithfulness with thousands and thousands.

With this Hope, I put myself to study, and hope sustained me through many years of seminary. Hope helped me to see myself as a missionary rather than a refugee.

It is this Hope that lifts our spirits when we are discouraged, and when we are trapped in darkness, hope points us to light. When we are tempted to quit, Hope keeps us going. When we are afraid of tomorrow, Hope reminds us that God will be there when we reach tomorrow.

We cannot stay focused on the road to fulfill our dreams without hope.
Without hope we will all succumb to depression and despair. So friends, I invite you to hope again: when the fear of the unknown knocks at your door, hope again. When disappointment

meets you half way through the journey, hope again. When you are confused and discouraged, hope again. When your dreams fade, hope again.

The kind of hope I am talking about is brought about only by faith. It is useless to hope without faith. Hope points to the destiny, but it is faith that takes you there.

Since I do not know what you hope for and what your faith is founded on, let me tell you the source of mine. His name is Jesus Christ, the Son of the living God. He is my help, my refuge, my strong tower, and the rock of my salvation. He is my husband. He is my provider and protector, the author and finisher of my faith. He is the source of my confidence, in whom I will always put my trust and HOPE.

Anita, Axelle, Arlette, Arrielle, my daughters,
June, 2017 at Axelle's college graduation

With my daughters, September, 2017

Chapter Seventeen—Psalm 40

The time came after my husband left, that the girls grew up and two of them graduated from college and were getting married. The third daughter was in her last year of college and the baby was entering college. I was left alone with a dog.

We had been in our house for more than 15 years. It was our home. The girls grew up there, made friends, and we had memories in that house. At Christmas the previous year, all my daughters were home for the holiday and they talked me into thinking about moving into a smaller place. They knew how isolated I felt living alone in that big house. It was depressing to find myself alone and they knew it. This was a sign. I had prayed that the Lord would prepare them for the changes we were going to endure. I guess they were ahead of the game!

In the middle of June, my oldest daughter flew from Denver, Colorado, to Nashville to help me get the house ready for sale. She was exhausted and fell asleep on the upstairs couch in the place we used to call the "upper room." About 3:40 P.M., (we had been working since 8:00 A.M.) the heat was intense. The attic felt like an oven. Through the small entrance to the attic, I could see Arlette curled up on the couch under the ceiling fan, a bag of chips on the floor, and a cup of what was meant to be ice already melting and leaving the cup dripping on the glass table. As I watched her sleeping, my mind took me back to many years of a journey that started with an underage pregnant orphan. There, before my eyes, was the daughter from that pregnancy, a young woman who was well established as the owner of a condominium in Denver, Colorado, working on her master's degree—a hard-working, ambitious, young woman. Who would have guessed what the future held? My thoughts went far back to the many uncertain situations we faced; the fear, poverty, sickness, and moments when I didn't know what to do. She interrupted me: "How are we doing Mama?"

Standing in the attic, I forgot about the heat. I jumped back to reality and heard myself saying, "Almost done, Honey. We are almost out of this." It sounded unreal and it was. There I was in the middle of a huge mess! Boxes of school projects, books, out-grown shoes and clothes, Christmas ornaments, and everything else surrounded me. In one of the old suitcases, I found the little outfits and shoes the girls wore when we came to America. Arlette made a joke out of this discovery. "This was in style, Mom. You really tried!" We laughed a lot as we separated items into two piles (trash and Goodwill). I then realized that this was our story. We made 23 trips to Goodwill and each trip felt like one step out of the mess. A few weeks later she flew back to Denver, the house was on the market, and we had a couple of offers to choose from.

We held hands in the almost empty house and she looked at me with tears in her eyes and said, "Mama, I pray that you will be able to leave all this behind and move on to whatever God has for your next chapter." She went on praying for inner healing and strength for all of us, and that out of the sale of the house we would make enough to cover all our expenses and that we would get out of all financial chains and have a clean start somewhere else.

She prayed for things I thought I had kept from their knowledge, trying not to worry them. This broke me down as I realized that I was not alone in this mess. They (the girls) understood my fear and worries and even my weaknesses.

I felt vulnerable at this moment and I knew that if I didn't keep it together, she was going to miss her flight. She was sobbing and I lost control of my emotions as I considered her growth in the words she chose to use to uplift me.

My two middle daughters were at the University of Tennessee in Knoxville. They were not able to come home and help with this transition, and I was thankful for the Lord's wisdom that they weren't. It was emotional to trash the items that once we held precious— souvenirs of our lives in different places and moments that marked our journey. I am glad that they didn't have to be the ones to decide what to take and what to leave behind.

One night, around three in the morning, I was awakened by a familiar presence—a comforting and gentle presence, and a Word was imprinted on my heart when I woke up from that inexplicable moment. (Deuteronomy 2:3) "You have skirted this mountain long enough; turn northward." I knew then that the Lord had commanded me to move and change the direction of my life.

My realtor and I worked almost around the clock to get the house ready for inspection and appraisal. Yes, it was emotionally tearing; it was physically exhausting, but I had the Word! We became so dear to each other throughout this process that my daughter wound up marrying her son, so we really became family.

A few months prior to this moving process, I had applied for a position within the company I worked for. With the stress of moving and the changes I was going through, I forgot about it, and one day I received an email from my boss asking if I was still interested in the position. If "yes", I needed to email my new resume. I did and an interview was set. I landed the job!

There is a TV show called "Extreme makeover." I used to watch it and was always amazed by how these guys would transform old, almost abandoned houses and make them into beautiful homes with little changes on the outside. They would retouch the inside, reorganizing rooms and putting in valuable appliances and furniture for the extreme make over!

We also speak of God as a God of many chances. I got to taste an extreme makeover from the mighty hand of God! I, also, was given a chance to redo my life. Call it a second chance!

The room was brightened by the sunlight filtering through the window's blinds. I struggled to collect my thoughts. I didn't remember where I was and why I was there. The aches in my body from the hectic move brought me back to reality. I was not in a hotel room. I was right there in my new place. My heart started racing as usual. Fear tried to move in with me! The smell of a "brand new" home with all new furniture and all updated appliances spoke against fear!

The following weeks and months I learned to retrain my way of thinking. I had been on "auto-pilot" for so long avoiding thinking. No one had ever told me how hard thinking can become! Thinking was hurting my head! I literally fought to keep my mind in one place.

"Don't look back...Do not dwell on the past...I am doing a new thing!" I kept sensing this calming and comforting sweet voice. I later found it in Isaiah 43:18-19.

Looking back is a familiar gesture. Our human minds store memories and images of places and circumstances. It is easy to retrieve these past memories and feed on them, especially when you are bearing marks—scars that testify about your past life's experiences.

My past had so much power over me that even when I got some breakthrough, I didn't know what to do with freedom. I always expected things to go wrong, or people to walk away from me. I was suspicious about the generosity of new people in my life. It was too good to be true!

I found myself at a junction of an old life and a new single life that I never prepared for; from a full household of six members to a single "me." This downsized my financial responsibilities as well, which helped me leave the hundred jobs I was doing to make ends meet. I focused on one main job and started working on the writing of this book. I resumed my crafting skills that were forgotten for so long.

Sitting on my front porch on a beautiful Saturday morning, while writing this last chapter, it is indeed the beginning of spring! My front yard is recovering from the winter's harsh coldness. Dead plants are regaining strength, but signs of death are still visible on the outer parts of each tree and even in the grass. Though the inner part has been regenerated, the outer part still has a long way to go in order to reflect the original beauty.

It is at that moment when a dream is too good that you wish not to wake up! There is a peace and joy that I never knew I had room for in my heart—a mixture of feelings and an unspeakable happiness.

Throughout my journey, I may say, I came to understand that God always answers our heart's cries in three clear ways: Yes, No, and Wait. Although many of us do not understand these ways by which He (God) choses to answer our prayers and petitions, in my little experience, I found out that God came through in my troubles and many times He responded by "WAIT." I had no other option but to "wait".

"I waited patiently for the Lord;
And He inclined to me,
He also brought me up out of a horrible pit,
Out of the miry clay, and set my feet upon
a rock,
And established my steps." (Psalm 40:1-2)

Looking back to my struggles, I see clearly that my life had known so many ups and downs that it made it hard to give testimony for the few victories I experienced. For every victory I tasted, there was always a heartbreaking event that was waiting around the corner—a joy-snatching situation that always came to shut off my testimony. I lived in a horrible, dark, slippery pit!

"How long, O Lord?" This was my faithful prayer/cry.

It seemed that the only response was, "Never," according to Satan, the enemy of God's elect. This word stirred the deepest fear in my heart all of my life. At many points, my hope was gone. I lost the ability to dream like other girls and women do. I stopped wishing!

Waiting on God is a big challenge that requires supernatural grace—the grace that gives the ability to keep hoping when the "never's" of life push and knock at the door of our hearts and when the minutes and hours, days and years, tick away without any answers to our most ardent pleas at the throne of grace.

The grace that helps our faith to hang on to the Lord on the long road, when human reason tells us to give up, this grace is the expectant endurance.

I learned that there is a purpose in waiting; waiting is not wasting time. It is a call, a plea from God for His agenda that is not like ours, His timing is perfect. He is never early nor late. How do I know this? I know because while in that horrible pit, I studied what scripture has to say about it.

- "O my God, in You I trust… Indeed, none of those who wait for You will be ashamed." (Psalms 25:2-3)
- "Wait for the Lord; be strong and let your heart take courage; yes, wait for the Lord. (Psalms 27:14)
- "Don't be impatient for the Lord to act! Keep traveling steadily along his pathway and in due season he will honor you with every blessing." (Psalms 37:34, TLB)
- "My soul, wait in silence for God only, for my hope is from Him. He only is my rock and my salvation, my stronghold; I shall not be shaken." (Psalms 62:5-6)
- "The Lord favors those who fear Him, those who wait for His loving-kindness." (Psalms 147:11)
- "The Lord longs to be gracious to you, and therefore He awaits on high to have compassion on you. For the Lord is a God of Justice; how blessed are those who long for Him." (Isaiah 30:18)
- "Those who wait on the Lord will gain new strength; they will mount up with wings like eagles, they will run and not get tired, they will walk and not become weary." (Isaiah 40:31)

- " You will know that I am the Lord; those who hopefully wait for Me will not be put to shame." (Isaiah 49:23)
- "From days of old they have not heard or perceived by ear, nor has the eye seen a God beside You, who acts in behalf of the one who waits for you." (Isaiah 64:4)
- "The vision is yet for the appointed time; it hastens toward the goal and it will not fail. Though it tarries, wait for it; for it will certainly come, it will not delay." (Habakkuk 2:3)
- "Hope that is seen is not hope; for who hopes for what he already sees? But if we hope for what we do not see, with perseverance we wait eagerly for it." (Romans 8: 24-25)

These are only a few of the verses, but you get the point. Time is one of God's most effective tools for teaching us to rely on Him completely. This has been true throughout history—seen often in the lives of the greatest saints such as Abraham, Joseph, and David. It will be true to whosoever wants God's best until time itself is no more.

Waiting on God means remaining in your present circumstances until you receive further instructions and His intervention. I remained there in the miry clay. I had no options, but to remain. Even when I attempted to climb out of the pit I would make two steps out and fall back five steps! He made me wait. His grace pushed me back, keeping me from aborting the perfect plans He had for me and my daughters.

The 40th psalm speaks directly to my life's journey. I can't find any other way to explain my ups and downs than the scene of a horrible pit and being in miry clay!

> "He has put a new song in my mouth.
> Praise to our God;
> Many will see it and fear,
> And will trust in the Lord."
> (Psalm 40:3)

A song is never seen; a song is heard! How can we understand the wisdom of God in this scripture?

The truth was, as the unseen transforming power of spring comes into every plant, I was undergoing the same process. There was this restoring power that for a while had been piecing together my brokenness, though the outer, physical body was still the same! I still had scars and aches in my body—the back pain that would not heal, if not for the grace of God. This was part one of the song! It began in my soul, it brought hope as the healing took place in the hidden places of my heart, and it changed my life from the inside out.

For a long time I had been looking at life through a window, when sitting there under the morning sun, I couldn't believe it; I was out of the darkness; I was among the living!

One of my daughters just graduated from college and is married to the best son-in-law I ever prayed to have. The other one is half way done with her master's studies and is soon getting married to a wonderful young man. The third is in her last year of college, and the youngest just got into the University of Tennessee—each one working hard to get ahead.

The song broke out as the restoration of God's goodness was taking place in many physical areas of our lives. All who know my daughters and me will see it. No words are needed to sing my song—the song of praise to my God, the Mighty one whose hand reached out and rescued us.

Out of the horrible pit! A new song in my heart is being seen. It's a song of praise to my God. It is inspired by faith which brings hope;

hope to welcome and love new sons-in-law, hope to love and cherish grandchildren, hope to dream, and hope to serve the Lord and hope to dare to love again. Why not?

"Through It All"
by Andréa Crouch

I've had many tears and sorrows,
I've had questions for tomorrow.
There's been times I didn't know right from
wrong.
But in every situation,
God gave me blessed consolation,
That my trials come to only make me strong.

Through it all,
Through it all,
I've learned to trust in Jesus,
I've learned to trust in God.

Through it all
Through it all
I've learned to depend upon His Word

I've been to lots of places
I've seen a lot of faces,
There's been times I felt so alone.
But in my lonely hours,
Yes those precious lonely hours,
Jesus lets me know that I was His own

Through it all,
Through it all,
I've learned to trust in Jesus,
I've learned to trust in God.

Through it all,
Through it all,
I've learned to depend upon His Word.

Appendices/Maps

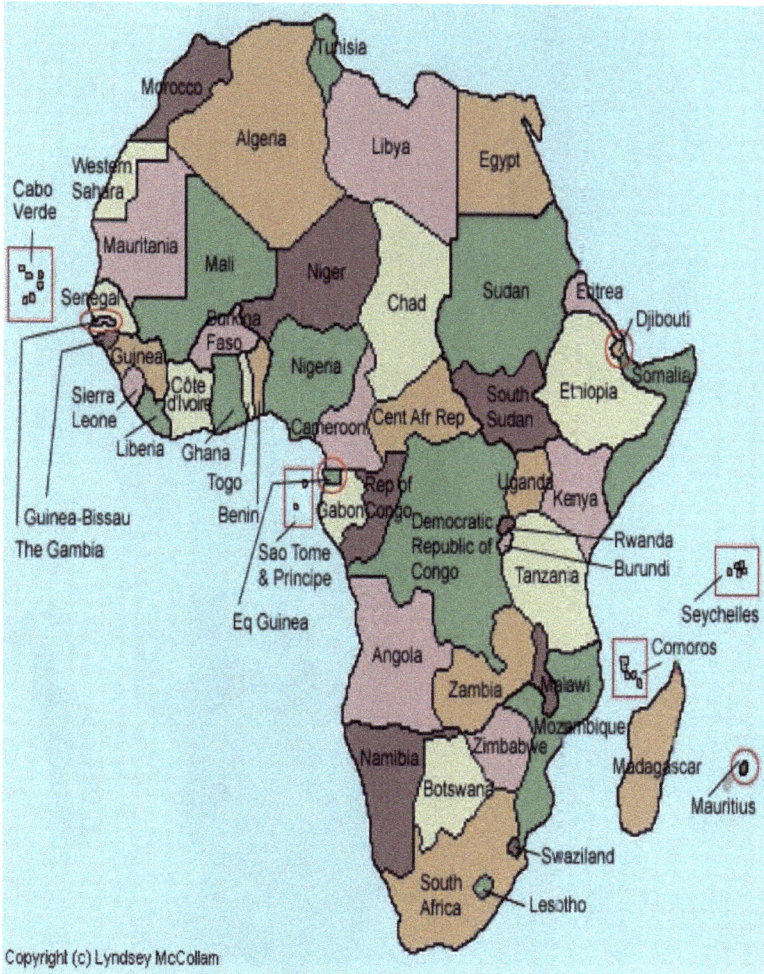

Copyright (c) Lyndsey McCollam

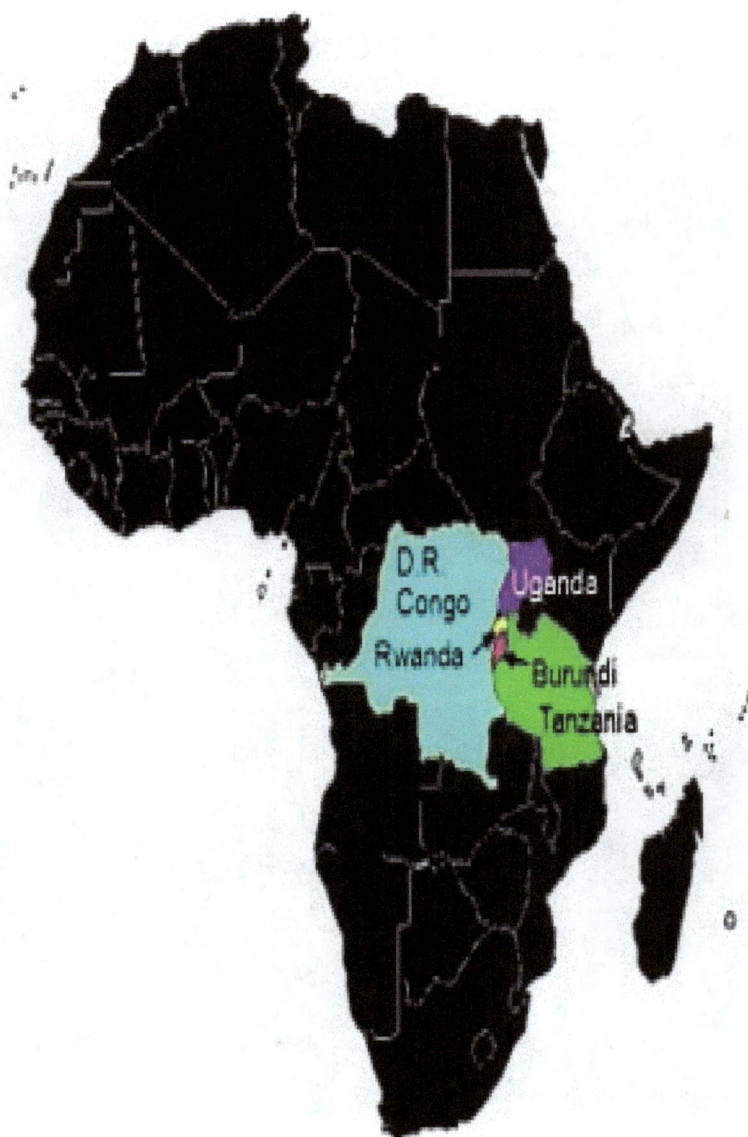

D.R. Congo
Uganda
Rwanda
Burundi
Tanzania

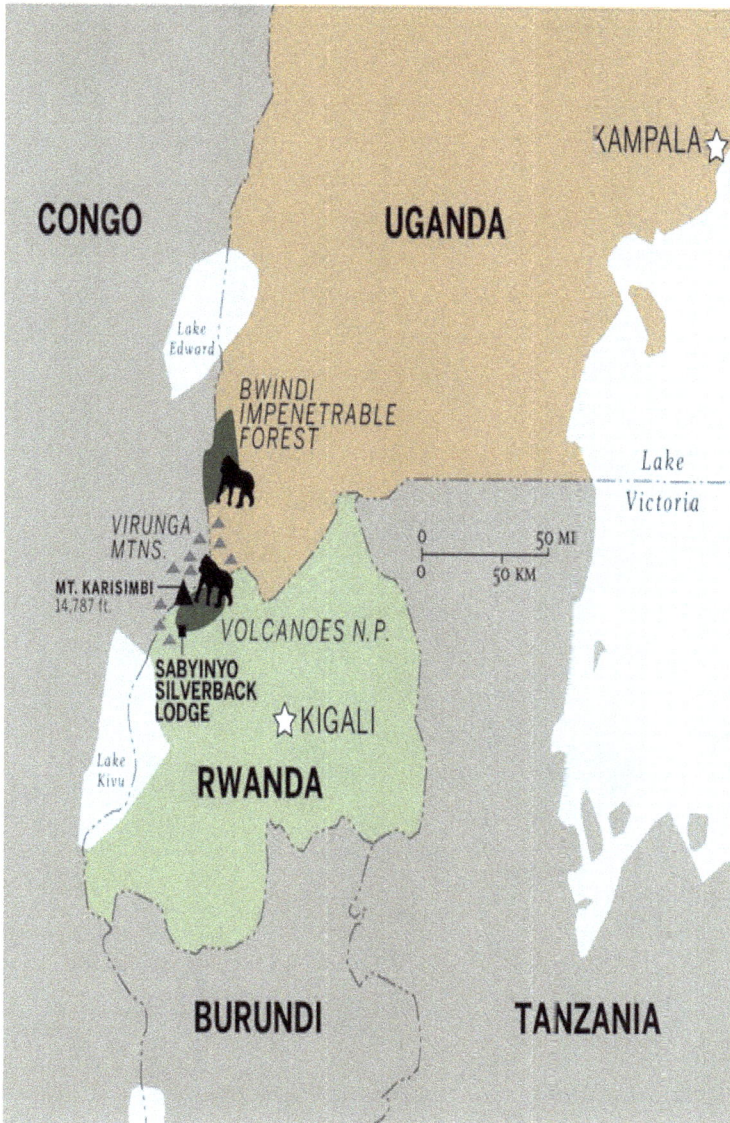

CONGO

UGANDA

KAMPALA ☆

Lake
Edward

BWINDI
IMPENETRABLE
FOREST

Lake
Victoria

VIRUNGA
MTNS.

MT. KARISIMBI
14,787 ft.

VOLCANOES N.P.

SABYINYO
SILVERBACK
LODGE

0   50 MI
0   50 KM

☆ KIGALI

Lake
Kivu

RWANDA

BURUNDI

TANZANIA

Uganda, Rwanda, Burundi

	International Boundary
	Road
	Minor Road
	River
★	National Capital
•	City or Town

0   150 KM

0   150 Miles

© 2007 Geology.com

Epilogue

After the genocide of 1994, the Rwandan people came together and rebuilt the country with unity and reconciliation. They recognized the horror of the genocide and resolved that it should never happen again. Some people made apologies and restitutions.

Rwanda today is a peaceful place in the entire continent of Africa. She is a pure image of God's restoring power. The unity and love of her people are admired by all. The nonprofit organization I founded, African Global Mission, has helped widows, and other survivors of the genocide war to gain skills and the ability to rebuild their lives and support their families through small home-based businesses. We invite the whole world to learn from this tragic story and to pray for the continued success of the Rwandan people and all others who suffer for injustice and the lack of leadership. May God continue to bless the Rwandan people and may He bless America as well.